CW01018190

LIVERPOOL
AND THE
'45 REBELLION

by

DON HIGHAM

A FACTUAL ACCOUNT OF THE INVASION BY BONNIE PRINCE CHARLIES HIGHLAND ARMY AND ITS EFFECT ON THE PEOPLE OF S. W. LANCASHIRE

First published 1995 by Countyvise Limited, 1 & 3 Grove Road, Rock Ferry, Birkenhead, Wirral, Merseyside L42 3XS.

Copyright © Don Higham, 1995.

ISBN 0 907768 79 2 Countyvise Limited.

Photoset and printed by Birkenhead Press Limited, 1 & 3 Grove Road, Rock Ferry, Birkenhead, Wirral, Merseyside L42 3XS.

ACKNOWLEDGMENT

Special Thanks to:-

I wish to thank DENNIS REEVES, curator of the Liverpool Scottish Museum who "introduced" me to the "Liverpool Blues", his enthusiasm, guidance and contributions helping immensely with the following pages.
JANET SMITH and STAFF at the Liverpool Record Office for their assistance also J. GORDON READ, curator, archives, Merseyside Museums.
SARAH BURDETT and DONNA HIGHAM for their typing and PC. work.
Also my wife for her patience, and friends for their encouragement over the years, all who helped to make this book possible.

Don Higham

FOREWORD

Of the mid 18th century, Picton said "we know more of Rome under the Emperor Augustus than we do of Liverpool". Perhaps the following pages will contribute a little to redress the balance.

Alternatively much has been written generally about the 1745 rebellion especially covering events in England and Scotland and the roles played by the leading characters of the day, Bonnie Prince Charlie and The Duke of Cumberland.

In the following pages I have emphasised the roles played by the "ordinary" people of Liverpool and the surrounding areas, and how and why these events affected them.

I have pushed the central figures of history into the background and let the "man in the street" take, for a change, centre stage.

DON HIGHAM

CHAPTER I

The Liverpool Ship "Ann" bucked and rode the mountainous waves off the west coast of Scotland. It was early August in the year 1745 and the weather for those parts was, as usual, unpredictable. She had come around the rugged Cape Wrath on short sail, her yard arms now pitching over and dragging through the seas.

The brigatine was carrying timber from Riga in Latvia on the Baltic Coast to her home port on the Mersey and was desperate for shelter.

The Captain, Richard Robinson, peering through the storm was able to distinguish the rocky shores of the Western Isles and pointed the jib through the jagged passages of unfriendly rocks and isles to the craggy offshore coastline of the mainland.

She came into calmer waters south of the Isle of Skye and dropped anchor between the Isle of Canna and Loch Nan Uamh.

The crew could now relax somewhat on the gently heaving waves and await a change in the direction of the winds. The journey around the Orkneys had been heavy going and they were thankful for the rest.

The Captain and some crew members went ashore for victuals keen to learn of any developments regarding the war in Europe.

They were guarded in their enquiries appreciating that the loyalties of many of the inhabitants in the isles would be in favour of the French, and in some cases, openly supporting the continental enemy.

Britain had experienced a long period of peace which came to an abrupt end when she declared war on Spain in 1739. Other countries rapidly became involved in this conflict which became known as the "War of the Austrian Succession" with Britain supporting Austria (the war lasting until 1748) but it was the arrival of the old enemy France into this theatre of war in the year 1742 which set the hopes soaring of the Jacobites in England and Scotland.

The French Government laid plans for a full scale invasion of Britain and the many critics of King George II's Hanoverian

1

government felt now the time had come to re-establish the Stuarts once more on the throne of England.

At various times in the early years of the 18th century, the French had organised a variety of invasion manoeuvres using Scotland to divert England's attention away from the European mainland. The latest plan was to support Prince Charles Edward Stuart, the grandson of James II, with a French army of 3,000 men landing them in the Scottish Highlands. The clans were to join them; they would then march on London gathering loyal English Jacobites enroute and finally an additional 12,000 men were to be landed near London for a final assault on the capital itself.

In 1744 a large French force was prevented from leaving Dunkirk by the British fleet assisted by fierce gales, which wrecked many French ships and transports, leading to the abandonment of the expedition.

The Prince considered it only a "postponement" and carried on with his plans to land in Scotland in the June of 1745. Many of his supporters were less than enthusiastic about these preparations; never-the-less, he sailed for Scotland with a few companions, an abundance of energy, arrogance and optimism.

His arrival on the 23rd July on the island of Eriskay off the West Coast of Scotland was met by his supporters with little zeal, but the 25 year old Prince was undeterred; 2 days later, he was anchored in Loch Nan Uamh on the Arisaig Coast where the reception this time was more favourable. The charisma of the Chevalier de St. George as he was known, was beginning to shine; it was the start of the legend of "Bonnie Prince Charlie".

Due to the remoteness of the western Highlands the Jacobites were able to organise the gathering of the clans, and in comparative secrecy, make preparations for a full scale rebellion.

Captain Robinson now discovered from the local people that a tall, handsome stranger had been conducting his affairs in the area and many people openly referred to him as "Prince Charles". The alarmed skipper cast off and hastily made full sail for the Mersey.

The "Ann" arrived in Liverpool late on the 15th August and the following day Captain Robinson rapidly made his way to the Exchange (Town Hall) to confer with the Mayor, Owen Pritchard, and the Corporation all the details regarding the landing and activities of the Prince on the coast of Scotland.

An affidavit and loyal letter of support was then sent to his Majesty (King George II) by express rider to the Secretary of State in London, the Duke of Newcastle.

The London Gazette, in a vague report on the 17th August, had reported a "sighting" on the west coast of the Pretender's son, but it was Captain Robinson's first hand report that brought confirmation to England that, in fact, Prince Charles had landed in Scotland and that a rising was in the process of being organised.

Liverpool to say the least was uneasy. The previous century had seen the small town ravaged by 3 sieges as parliamentarians and royalists in turn fought over the strategic port in the English Civil War.

The worst had seen the Liverpool parliamentarians defending their port and castle against Prince Rupert's experienced forces. The town had been strongly fortified with a high earthen wall to the north, a stockade to the east, to the west lay the River Mersey, the south was shielded by the old Pool itself.

Prince Rupert had looked down on the small besieged port from his encampment on Everton Hill and scoffed that the town was "a crows nest that may be taken by a parcel of boys", but after numerous assaults during which he lost 1,500 men over 18 days and his cannons had used up a 100 barrels of gunpowder, he was forced to admit that "it was more an eagles nest, or lions den". Nevertheless, his troops finally breeched the ramparts to the north near Old Hall and the royalist catholic soldiers, led by local landowner Caryl, brother of Lord Molyneux, "put many to the sword for hours and giving no quarter", "... a great company and the inhabitants being murdered and slain."

Caryl Molyneux allegedly killing 7 or 8 people personally.* The people of the small town had long memories.

This had taken place a 100 years previously, but only 30 years earlier, at the rising in support of the Stuarts in 1715**, a London newspaper "The Flying Post" reported that again:

---

* According to Moore's account

** In support of the Father of Prince Charles

3

"Liverpool had thrown up ditches, dammed up the Pool stream to form a protection to the east, they had arranged the ships in the river so as to give aid in defence, they cut a deep ditch from the river to the Pool along the edge of the old rampart (of the Civil War sieges) and on it entrenchments commanding the Pool. The streets were barricaded and 70 cannon ringed the town. These were manned by sailors, and 1,000 men were under arms and organised into companies, drilling and ready to defend the town."

An armed party of these volunteers at that time called at Croxteth Hall (the family seat of the Molyneuxs), gained access and took away loaded firearms. They took Lord Molyneux and another suspected Jacobite sympathiser to the jail at Liverpool Tower for questioning.

It was recorded that these military preparations took just 3 days to organise, illustrating the ability and efficiency of the town's people to unite when under threat. This capacity was again emphasised with the new calamity that was now imminent.

Liverpool by 1745 had developed in leaps and bounds reflecting its prosperity from a small fishing village in the 17th Century to a bustling mid-18th century town.

At this time the population was over 20,000 with the influx of Scots and Irish migrants; in fact, people from all the Irish Sea coastal areas seeking a share in the booming prosperity of the port. The town boundaries were now pushed eastwards onto the Great Heath, that rising moorland with its Gallows Mills standing like sentinels near the London Road, and to the south houses now stretched out, up the Park Lane into Toxteth Park and more houses straddled both sides of the Pool stream. The old Pool itself had now gone and a new dock constructed there in 1715.

This enclosed dock was the first development of its kind having been constructed as Liverpool became first a vigorous competitor to London and Bristol before rapidly surpassing Bristol. Author Daniel Defoe had earlier described the bustling town as a "Little London".

By 1745 there were 11 acres of docking area including the pier, which also acted as a breakwater for shipping, and lamps had been erected to light the area "enhancing the security of life and prosperity".

This prosperity however, created contrasts, the new overtaking the old. It meant that towering church spires, lofty windmills and fine warehouses stood alongside rotten wood frame houses, which threatened to touch across the narrow streets, and grand merchants' houses built of brick, adjacent to stone or wood cottages with thread bare thatching, five civic buildings with paved thoroughfares near tumbledown hovels propped up in earthen alleyways. It was certainly a town of stark architectural contrasts.

The population too, consisted of contrasts, living together side by side, rich and poor, dandies and beggars, rubbing shoulders and overspilling into each other's society.

The leaders of the community, the Liverpool merchants, were rich men, but unlike those of the country districts and even his counterparts of other ports, the Liverpool merchant was a self-made man, many had begun life as tradesmen or mariners. They had sailed and built ships, forming trading companies. They had explored the markets of the Mediterranean and sailed the Western Ocean and the Carribean Sea, up the coast of America bringing home rich harvests.

These merchants had transformed Liverpool from a sea going port into an ocean going one. Her merchants were comparable to those of London, they were "universal", but there the similarity ended. This rapid growth and development with trade flourishing caused resentment amongst the older, established merchant houses of London and Bristol. They took delight in satirising the "down to earth" qualities of the new merchant princes. A pamphlet published in London at the time mocked the manners and style of these Liverpool "gentlemen".

> "I co'd not chuse but think it strange
> To see so many rough hewn faces
> The saylors hitch in all their paces.
> Each merchant like tarpaulin moves
> As if he had no use for gloves."

The ditty goes on illustrating the object of their derision.

> Our business being much the same
> At length to Liverpoole we came
> And any man alive who'd guess.
> By the towns sudden rise no less
> From a small fishery of late
> Became the darling childe of Fate
> So wealthy grown so full of hurry
> That she eclipses Bristols glory."

Although Liverpool more than competed with other ports in conventional trade, she excelled in the African trade, the slave trade, but this business aside she was also master of the "privateer".

These were merchant vessels which, in the course of their normal voyages, had obtained a Letter of Marque from the government. This consisted of a certificate granting the ship authority to attack enemy vessels of the countries that England may be at war with.

Over the years these had developed into sleek craft, carrying cannon and swivel guns and their sailors gained a reputation for great daring on the high seas.

These ships had brought in much of the town's riches, destroying and capturing many Spanish and French ships (with little loss to her own), bringing home rich cargoes to be distributed proportionately amongst the ship's company, from the owners down to the young apprentices.

The whole town rejoiced when these prizes were brought into the Mersey, everybody eventually getting some portion of the booty. It has been recorded that "trade flourished and spread her golden wings" in this period.

What kind of men were they these Liverpool "men of the sea", these slavers and privateers? Most of the town's population had sea going knowledge; those who had retired or were invalids took up residence near the docks and involved themselves in business connected with the sea. Young boys would listen, spellbound, on the quayside to tales of combat, of ships locked in conflict, of adventures on the African coast and down the rivers of the dark continent to steal and barter for slaves. Then, full sail to New England or the Windward Isles, perhaps capturing a Spanish or French ship enroute.

They were a tough, hardy "no nonsense" breed, many becoming brutalised by the very nature of their work, which embraced the horror of slavery and the raw excitement of a French broadside.

A writer of the day speaking from personal observation about the crews of these private ships of war, described them thus:

> "The Captain was always some brave daring man who had fought his way to his position. The officers were selected for the same qualities, and the men, what a reckless, dreadnought dare-devil collection of human beings, half disciplined, but yet ready to obey every order, the more desperate the better,your true privateers man was a sort of half-horse, half-alligator, with a streak of lightning in his composition something like a Man-of-Wars man, but much more like a pirate, generally with a super abundance of whisker, as if he held with Sampson that his strength was in the quantity of his hair."

But "Jolly Jack" could be a ferocious ally. These men who dazzled the eyes and kindled the spirits of their fellow landsmen when ashore, would be fettered like heroes in the drinking dens and mean streets around the dock area. Here general rowdiness would often erupt into violence and violence into rioting as the mob would pursue some grievance, real or imaginery, fighting with cutlass and firearms, and it was not unknown for a merchant prince to take to the streets with pistols blazing, in an endeavour to protect his home and property, and shred his own thin veneer of respectability.

These rich merchants living within such close proximity to their less fortunate neighbours were to develop a social conscience, future generations of course would live outside the town, but in the mid 18th century the rich lived within the vicinity of drifters and migrants, drunks and adventurers as well as the everyday shopkeepers and tradesmen, attempting to make a respectable living.

This awareness stimulated their desire to build schools, a hospital, organise clubs and charities to assist the unfortunates who had been brushed aside by the town's boisterous prosperity.

Now was the time for the Liverpool people to put aside their social differences, the continental War had now arrived on British shores, albeit in the wild Highlands of north Britain, but the threat was looming ever closer: when would the French arrive to assist their Scottish allies?

In times of war Liverpool, as in the past, could not help but look over its shoulder just beyond the town boundaries and appreciate that they were completely encircled by a largely catholic population, where squires and landowners ruled their estates and countryside. Within 12 miles of the old tower it was estimated that there were 50 halls and secret chapels of the catholic gentry, many of the country people there would welcome a Stuart King, these were considered by many Liverpool people, if not "fifth columnists" at least a potential threat.

Liverpool had a deep mistrust of the landed gentry generally* and the catholic gentry in particular. Their recent history provoked this line of thought throughout the town, thus creating an isolationist mentality amongst the people. Although indifferent to the monarchy, a change in King could bring an end to its new found wealth and relative stability.

---

* Liverpool castle was a Molyneux stronghold and, because of past differences between the Corporation and the Molyneuxs, was razed to the ground when it was obtained by the town 1720c (as would be the Tower of the Stanleys in later years)

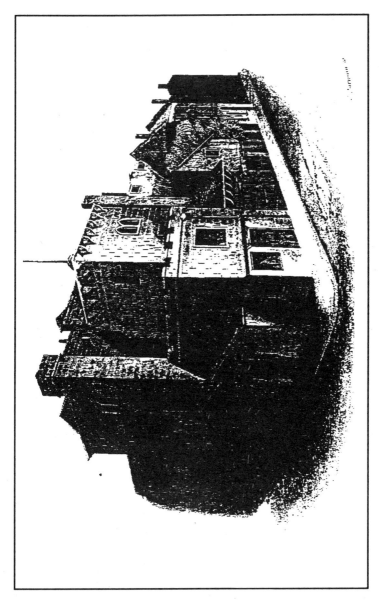

(Lv.R.O.)

Liverpool Tower
*Used as a guard-room armoury
assembly room and prison
during the emergency.*

CHAPTER II

Liverpool as in 1715 declared its loyalty - they were Hanoverian, Parliamentary, Whig Supporters and as far as the Government in London were concerned, would be the only reliable support in the County of Lancashire.

The town was getting anxious, the government had in fact heard "news" from Edinburgh regarding the rising as early as 8th August, but apparently not implemented any action to meet the storm clouds that were now gathering, certainly not as far as Liverpool was concerned.

The townsfolk gathered and the Corporation met to talk about the defence for the port. It was suggested they encircle the town with cannon, recruit volunteers and form a regiment to defend themselves as in previous emergencies.

It was now mid-September and an apprehensive Corporation called a special council meeting on the 17th deciding to send a Loyal Address to his Majesty.

1. As a declaration of their support and loyalty, and

2. In an endeavour to stimulate some action from the authorities.

TO THE KINGS'S MOST EXCELLENT MAJESTY

"The humble address of the Mayor, Recorder, Aldermen and Common Address. Council of the Borough and Corporation of Liverpoole in the County Palatine of Lancaster.

"Most Gracious Sovereign:

"We, your Majesty's most dutyfull and loyal subjects, the Mayor, Recorder, Aldermen and Common Council of the ancient Borough of Liverpoole in Council beg leave to congratulate your Majesty on your safe and happy return to your British dominions after having contributed so much to the election of an Emperor, and thereby to settle the peace of Europe.

"The taking of Cape Breton by your Majesty's forces is another event which will add to the glorys of your Majesty's reign, as it is an acquisition much wished for and of the highest importance, not only to the trade of these nations, but as it will remain a constant supply and nursery of seamen for your Royal Navy.

"This second daring attempt of the Pretender in Scotland we cannot think of but with the utmost abhorrence; and we do so with hearts full of the warmest loyalty assure your Majesty that we will at the hazard of our lives and fortunes exert ourselves in the support of the succession in your Majesty's royal house (as this Corporation with the greatest unanimity did on the rebellion in the year one thousand seven hundred and fifteen) against all opposers whatsoever. Your Majesty's mild and prudent government calls for our earnest testimonys of loyalty as subjects; the defence of our religion and the support of our laws require them of us as men. All concur to demand our prayers for a continuance of your Majesty's reign over a free people, and that the succession may remain in your Royal and Illustrious House to the latest posterity.

"In testimony whereof" etc.

This declaration was stamped with the Corporation seal and an express rider was appointed to go immediately to the capital, other young men volunteered and a squad organised as express riders for future duties. Fast horses were hired and put on standby and the coming months would see these express riders seeking out the various generals throughout the country who were organising the national army to obtain intelligence regarding the enemy strengths and their proposed route march south, through England and in fact any information to Liverpool's advantage. Amongst these express riders were:

Samuel Street	John Harrison
Thomas Stevenson	John Howard
Matthew Strong	James Wharton
Roger Carsley	John Ward
Jos. Hardwick	John Eyes

Liverpool also took stock of its public arms; an inventory confirmed the town held 4 chests containing 220 muskets, 1 chest containing 154 pistols, also there were 25 swords. The weapons were old but regularly maintained.

These were the arms of the Corporation normally reserved in case of public disorder.

In Scotland, Prince Charles had raised his standard at Glenfinnan on 19th August, his army then numbering just 1300 men.

By the 4th September, the Highland Army had marched into Perth, they left on the 11th September marching south. By the 17th of the month they had taken Edinburgh itself; by now their number was 2,550 men.This news reached Liverpool by express riders and the Corporation, feeling it had "sat back" long enough, promptly held a special council meeting on 21st September.

It was recorded.

> "Upon intelligence being received that the Pretender's son is now invading Scotland with a great force, and a plan being now laid before this Council for raising fortifications about this town for its defence against the rebels; and a subscription being proposed to be set on foot for the defraying of the expenses thereof. It is now Ordered that this Corporation do pay and contribute the sume of one thousand pounds towards the carrying on these works, and raising forces for the defence of the town; and that a Bond be passed under the Seal to any persons willing to advance 'em the money on the usual interest for a security for a repayment of the same; and that Ald. Steers have the direction of the works, and to call in any person to his assistance that he shall think necessary and proper. And the Corporation Committee to allow of and order the treasurer" pay the bills upon 'em being signed by Ald. Steers, "Ordered, That the Constables do give a list to the Mayor the preceding day, of persons who are to watch the next night; and that Mr. Pole to pay the watch who have watched these three nights last, past, twelve pence a piece a night. And for the future twenty five men to be hired to watch every night, and to be paid only eight pence a piece a night. And also that Ald. Brooke be empowered to hire and set a watch of six

men on the powder magazine till the powder be shipped on board some ship. And that Mr. Bird may hire two small vessels to take the powder on board and hire people to guard it.

"Ordered, that Mr. Deputy Mayor be empowered to dispatch Samuel Street for his intelligence to Edinburgh or any other places he shall think proper; and that the treasurer do advance him ten guineas towards his expenses."

Accordingly, Samuel Street rode out from the stables of Thomas Davies heading north up the Scotland road, while Jos. Hardwicke had the previous day (20th September) rode south with a letter from the Corporation to the Secretary of War voicing the fears and again expressing the loyalty of the town, indicating its wish for a Royal Warrant that would grant them power to form a military regiment.

Liverpool, impatient to get its defence arrangements under way, had instructed the express rider to deliver the Corporation's letter to the King, and await a reply before returning back to Liverpool.

From Whitehall on the 21st September Holles Newcastle, The Secretary of War had written to the Lords Lieutenants and Magistrates of the northern counties instructing them to organise and "call up" the county militia.

These Lords Lieutenants of the various counties were "The Kings Lieutenants of and in the County" with sub-Lieutenants under their authority.

The Government was well aware of the disjointed and ineffectiveness of the existing laws relating to the county militia acts at that time, but of course not wishing to admit their own past failures in this sphere, passed the onus onto the Lords Lieutenants in the hope that they may arrive at an eventual solution but if not, the failure would reflect on the county administration rather than central government.

The Secretary for War wrote on the 21st September to the 1st Lieutenant of Cheshire, Lord Cholmondeley, informing him that he and the other 3 Lords Lieutenants of the northern counties were being issued with appropriate warrants to call up the militia, explaining the current situation in Scotland and requested (somewhat desperately) suggestions for other methods for recruitment of volunteers.

There were no shortages of volunteers in Liverpool and in the War Secretary's letter to the Deputy Mayor he congratulated the town on its state of readiness. He also explained the latest information he had regarding the English forces, as he had done to the Lords Lieutenants in his letters to them.

Mr. Brooke
The Deputy Mayor

"Sir,

"I received yesterday, by express, your letter of the 20th inst. and have laid it before the King; who extremely approved the zeal and attention to his service, which you and the other Magistrates of Leverpoole have shewn in the present critical conjuncture, and the precautions you have taken for putting that town into a condition of defence.

"I send you enclosed a Warrant, under His Majesty's Royal Sign Manual, directed to the Mayor of Leverpoole, (which you will deliver to him) authorising, and empowering him, to form into Troops, or Companies, such of the inhabitants as shall be willing to take arms; and to grant Commissions to such persons as he shall think proper to exercise, and command them. The like powers have been granted by His Majesty, in several Counties, on occasion of the present Rebellion; and to the Mayors of Berwick, Carlisle and Newcastle. And His Majesty is persuaded that this trust, which he had thought fit to repose in the principle Magistrate of Leverpoole, The Mayor, will be executed in such a manner, as shall most effectually contribute to the support of His Majesty's Government; the preservation of the Publick Peace, and the disappointment of the attempts and designs, of the Pretender, and his adherants.

"We are in hopes, the next letters from Scotland, will bring an account, that Sir John Cope has been able effectually to stop the progress of the rebels. But if contrary to our expectations, they should find means, without coming to an engagement with His Majesty's forces, to march into England, Sir John Cope is at full liberty to follow them.

Lieut-General Wentworth with two Dutch Regiments, (amounting to 2,200 men), five Companies of Blakeney's Regiment, The Duke

Mr. Brooke
Depty Mayor of Liverpoole.

Whitehall. Sept. 23. 1745.

Sir,

I received yesterday, by
Express, Your Letter of the 20th Inst.
and have laid it before the
King; who extremely approves
the Zeal, & Attention to His
Service, which You, and the
other Magistrates of Leverpole
have shew'd in the present
critical Conjuncture, and the
Precautions You have taken
for putting that Town into a
Condition of Defence.

I send You inclosed a
Warrant, under His Majesty's
Royal Sign Manual, directed
to the Mayor of Leverpoole, &
(which You will deliver to Him
authorising, and Empowering
Him, to form into Troops, or
Companies, such of the
Inhabitants, as shall be
willing to take arms; and to
grant Commissions to such
Persons, as He shall think prope

Portion of letter from Holles Newcastle
Secretary for war, authorising recruiting of troops.

Public Record Office

of Montague's Regiment of Horse, and Brig'r St. George's Regiment of Dragoons; is on his march towards Lancashire, or to any other part of England, where he shall hear the rebels are.　　Two other Dutch Regiments, which arrived in the River of Thames on Friday last, were ordered to proceed forthwith by sea to Newcastle. "I have the pleasure to acquaint you, that yesterday the transports arrived from Williamstadt, with ten Regiments from our army in Flanders; amounting to upwards of 7,000 effective men.

You will receive from the Lords Comm'rs of the Admiralty an answer to your request, that the gun-powder at Leverpoole may be put on board the two Ships of War now lying there. As you will see, it is Their Lords opinion, that it is not practicable to secure the gun-powder proposed, on board those ships, I am glad to find, that the proper directions are sent by this express, by the persons concerned in London, to their correspondents at Leverpoole, for hiring a vessel, on which it may be immediately put on board, if necessary, which vessel will be under the protection of His Majesty's Ships of War.

His Majesty has it under consideration in what manner his loyal subjects at Leverpoole may be supply'd with arms; and I will soon send you an account of what can be done in it.

I am ..... etc.

Holles Newcastle
Whitehall

The attached Warrant read:
His Majesty's Royal Sign Manual and Commission to the Mayor.

"George the Second, by the grace of God King of Great Britain etc. "To our trusty and well beloved Owen Pritchard Mayor of our town of Liverpoole in Lancashire, Greeting.

"Whereas several of our loyal subjects in our town of Leverpoole have testified unto us their earnest desire in time of common danger when a rebellion is actually begun within this our kingdom in favour of a Popish Pretender, to enter into associations for taking up arms for the common defence, and have desired our Royal approbation and authority for their so doing.

"We therefore having a just sense of so commendable a zeal, and being desirous to encourage this seasonable instance of their loyalty

16

to us, and their concern for the religion and libertys of their country, have thought it fit hereby to give you power and authority, and we do hereby authorize and empower you to signifye to our well affected subjects our Royal approbation of the said design, and to form into troops or companys such persons as shall be willing to associate themselves for the purposes aforesaid in our town of Liverpoole; and to grant Commissions in our name to such of them as you shall think proper to exercise and command them.

And for your executing and performing the power and authority hereby given and granted to you, this shall be a sufficient warrant.

"Given at our Court at Kensington this 23rd day of September 1745 in the nineteenth year of our reign.

By His Majesty's Command Holles Newcastle.

"The Mayor, Leverpoole to grant Commissions."

Liverpool now had its Royal Warrant enabling the corporation to recruit soldiers and the Mayor to grant Commissions for Officers. It was the only town from Carlisle to the Mersey and west of the Pennines to offer an organised defence.

Liverpool had anticipated the deteriorating situation. The day after their request for a Royal Warrant, Sir John Cope's army had been defeated at Prestonpans on 21st September, all Scotland was now in the hands of the Jacobites; Charles now considered his Highlanders invincible.

The victory encouraged other clans and individuals to join the Princes army, they came over from the Western Isles, the mountains and glens of the north, from the townships of mid-Scotland and even lowlanders south of the highland line came to join the Scottish army.

The English Government reeled in horror at the shock defeat, and the formerly complacent English public was suddenly catapulted into action as they appreciated that the threat of invasion was now very real.

Demonstrations of support for King and Country were illustrated by the formation of defence groups across the land. People wrote to the press, sermons were preached from the pulpits of the churches, and money was publicly subscribed for town defences as the people of England geared themselves for action. Apart from the county militias, other volunteer groups sprang up throughout the country. The majority of these being formed by the local gentry in their respective areas.

Because of the disarray with the county militia's position, the Government now had no choice but to respond to any suggestion by other parties; town militias under the jurisdiction of the senior magistrate (the Mayor) being an option open to them.

It was these units which the Government hoped to use as auxiliary soldiers to support the regular army.

Edward Earl of Derby, 1st Lord of Lancashire, had received his letter at Knowsley on 26th September from Holles Newcastle (a few days later than the others) perhaps the delay in sending had been an oversight. Nevertheless, Lord Derby fully conversant with the current emergency and his responsibilities, had already journeyed up to Preston and convened a meeting of the gentry which included the sub-Lieutenants of Lancashire, the object being to organise the militia and raise a subscription.

The militia system required every able bodied man in the county to be balloted for "call-up", every parish having to submit a proportional number of men for duty, these supposedly trained men were escorted to the militia head quarters, with them muskets supplied and maintained by their own parish.

Lord Derby, absolutely loyal to the King (though not being one to associate with those at court) was becoming increasingly exasperated by the bureaucracy which restricted the organisation of the militia, the lack of financial support from the Government, and the petty bickering amongst the Lancashire gentry.

He wrote to his friend, Lord Cholmondeley at Chester Castle on 29th September regarding the Preston meeting:-

> "...£5,000 was received by subscription, yet I hope it may be double the sum when it has gone through the county, if the Government approves the proposals on which it is grounded, besides this, the town of Liverpoole by leave under his Majesty's Sign Manual have intaken to raise 1,000 men and a letter last night informs me that the number have already entered their names, thus things stand at present in this county

18

where the regular troops are much (called) for. By the recital you are please to give of His Grace of Newcastles letter to your Lordship, I find it the same that he honored me with and fancy the like has been sent to all other His Majesty's Lieutenants, some sooner some later.

"That your Lordship had not earlier notice of the associations carrying on especially as you are in town (London) and the Privy Council where I thought such things were approved and settled must be to me a matter of surprise, that I should be forgot is no wonder, having never had any interest and very little acquaintance among the "Great Ones". However what I can do for the service of my King and country shall never be wanting, I am with the greatest respect my Lord, your most obedient servant-

Derby."

Lancashire's first Lieutenant had also written to the Privy Council complaining about the raw state and ill-clad militia, regretting that there was not a more efficient national militia, kept ready and financed by the Government; of course, it was too late to consider it by this time. He was further concerned that the troops, when formed, would be without arms, "as there are only 20 muskets in the county, save what maybe is in the hands of the Merchants of Liverpool".

The objects of these militia men was certainly not to engage with the enemy, their role being more fitting to that of a police keeping force. They could break up roadways in an endeavour to impede the enemy's progress and to generally assist any of the Government forces, but if it proved impossible for the militia to act accordingly, specific orders were laid down to disband them and to prevent their arms falling into the hands of the enemy.

In truth there was no way the Lancashire militia would reach even this basic standard with many people condemning the subscription calling it an illegal tax. Lord Derby himself had no legal powers to extract any money towards a subscription, and certainly none was forthcoming from the Government. It meant in reality and legally that the militia had 14 days pay; no wonder Lord Derby was concerned!

Concerned also was Thomas Bretherton, the Member of Parliament for Liverpool, he wrote to the Secretary of State suggesting that "if the rebels were to march for Kelso, it may well be apprehended, their design is to take the same route into Lancashire as the rebels did in 1715". He was voicing the concern of many   Liverpool folk. It was quite possible that the French could plan a landing in Wales or even on the Lancashire coast, particularly as the Jacobites were relying on the support of the north west.

This then was the position. If the Highland army did decide to march through Lancashire, and it appeared likely, then they could virtually march unopposed throughout the length of the county.

General George Wade, the Officer commanding the North East forces, would have to cut across the Pennines to intercept them. If this were not possible there would be no government soldiers at all in the county (the militia could be disregarded). Only Liverpool was organising a defence strategy and a regiment to oppose the rebels.

The usual turbulent town was now only too aware that they may be in the direct path of the oncoming Scots and were feverishly entering their names on the regimental muster lists. William Lee had been elected as recruiting officer, and accompanied by an Andrew Glover incessantly pounding on the "recruiting" drum in traditional fashion, they toured the taverns, providing potential volunteers with liberal quantities of ale, paid for by the Corporation to encourage as many as possible to sign. The short listing would come later and obviously those with military experience would be given preference.

There was no shortage of those willing to sign; they came from all occupations and age groups and it was not only the local townspeople, men came in from the villages and parishes outside of town, volunteers, like old soldier Robert Molyneux of Aughton, whose parish paid his wife an "allowance" whilst he was with the Liverpool regiment.

Ex-officers and retired NCO's came along to offer their expertise in training and drilling the men. Merchant men and Ships Officers volunteered their services, mariners would exchange the discipline of the sea for the discipline of the new regiment.

John Johnson*, 39 years old, baptist minister from the chapel in Byrom Street, offered his services, he was one of the local "fire and brimstone" preachers who thundered out raw sermons from the town pulpits. They were as political as they were religious. Most regiments in the service of the King had a minister accompanying them so Mr. Johnson offered to join in that capacity.

Also renowned for his fiery sermons at this time was preacher, John Brekell, he also could whip up his congregation into a fever of patriotism. One sermon extolled the virtues of "taking up arms against an unchristian enemy" and "to smite those who would make us slaves" (this to a town of slavers). Mr. Brekell was officially recognised after the emergency by the corporation for his loyal fervour and encouragement to his fellow townsmen.

Amongst the volunteers was an ex-soldier Walter Shairpe, he was commissioned as a Lieutenant and was able to assist with the training of new recruits. He also wrote an account of his experience with the new regiment, recording the day to day activities, frustrations, fatigues and humour of the Liverpool men.

Originally it was decided that there would be volunteers for 6 companies, comprising of 100 men in each, but this was eventually altered upon the arrival of the Commanding Officer.

By the 29th September, the broad outline of the force was formed and although in its early days the name sometimes varied, it was finally decided that the volunteers would be known as "The Royal Liverpool Regiment of Blues".

The Liverpool Blues, as they became known, was the first regiment in England to be named after its town of origin.

This flurry of activity in these last days of September resulted in the Mayor sending the following letter via express rider to the War Office on the 29th September:

"My Lord,

"Some urgent affairs calling me into Wales for a week, the cares of this Town was in the hand of Mr. Alderman Brookes, who served the office of Mayor this preeceding year; from whose zeal for the present Government Your Grace may be assured all

---

* John Johnson, a non-conformist preacher, was born at Lostock near Manchester. He became the founder of the sect termed the "Johnsonian Baptists" where he eventually preached from a chapel in Mathew Street.

imaginable care was taken in the preservation of the
publick peace and guarding in the best manner against
the desperate and traitorous designs now appearing
in open rebellion; from his hand I received the Sign
Manual His Majesty has been pleased to honour us
with, which trust I entreat Your Grace to be persuaded
shall be discharged by us as becomes the most dutiful
and loyal subject.

"The first step taken on this important occasion, was
consulting the Magistrates and His Majesty's other
loyal subjects here, in what manner we could most
effectively contribute to the support of his Majesty's
Government; the preservation of the publick peace
and the disappointment of the attempts and designs
of the Pretender and his adherants; and we were all
of the opinion that would best be done by raising 800
or 1,000 men, to march with others that may be raised
in the County, to join his Majesty's forces that came
into these parts; for when we came to survey the
length and situation of our Town it was found
impracticable to be fortified or indeed to be defended
with less than ten thousand men.

"The foregoing resolution being taken I had a
meeting yesterday of part of the inhabitants by whom
a voluntary Subscription was immediately entered
into of near three thousand pounds, which I have not
the least room to doubt will be considerably enlarged
at another meeting appointed for that purpose
tomorrow; and that we propose to form eight hundred
or a thousand men into Companies of one hundred
each, to fit them new blew frock coats, hatts, shoes
and stockings and to maintain them for two months
certain. I will pursuant to the power given me by his
Majesty's Royal Sign Manual appoint Captains,
Lieutenants and Ensigns over them and have afforded
the command of the whole to our worthy
Representative, Thomas Brereton Esq., (Member of
Parliament), as no one could be so agreeable to our
inhabitants; but he having declined so important a
trust, on account of his inexperience in the military

function, I must humbly entreat Your Grace to move His Majesty, that he will be graciously pleased to order some Colonel or other officer of known experience to come here and take the command of these Companies which we doubt not of having formed and cloathed in three weeks, near that number having already entered their names.

"I must also further desire Your Grace will be pleased to move his Majesty that we may be furnished with ammunition and arms for such a number of men, which shall be returned into his Majesty's magazines when the occasion of having had them shall happily cease.

"It is with very great concern we see this defeat of the force under Sir John Cope near Edinburgh; but I can take upon me to assure Your Grace that it rather animates than abates the zeal of his Majesty's loyal subjects in Liverpoole, who are determined to lose the last drop of their blood in the defence of his Majesty's undoubted title to the crown of these realms.

"I have only to add that I will appoint some persons to be officers in the Companys who have already behaved well in his Majesty's service, the others will come from young gentlemen of this town who have some time payed old Sergeants to instruct them in the Military Exercise.

"The arrival of so many of our forces from abroad, and the expectation of more, gives us a most sensible pleasure, which would still be encreased could we promise ourselves that his Majesty would be pleased to send for some of his Hanoverian troops to assist his British Force in this time of imminent danger.

"I have the honour to be,
My Lord
Your Grace's Most Obedient &
Most Faithful Servant   (Owen Pritchard)

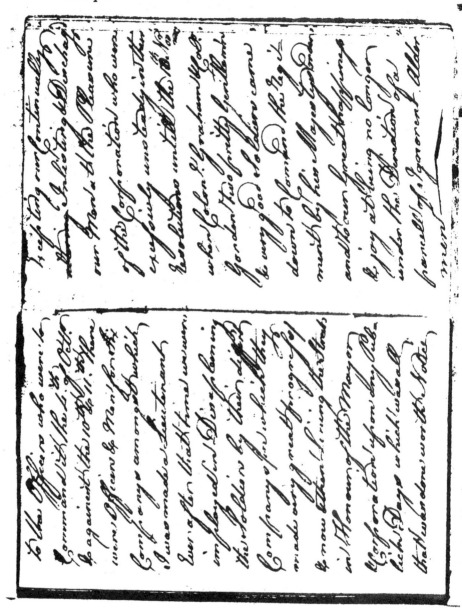

Lt. Shairpe's Diary
An extract from his account

The defensive position was coming together although the town had decided that, unlike previous times, it was now not practical to defend Liverpool with stockades and ditches, some fortifications to defend important establishments were organised, canons were brought into the Customs House yard and positioned on the roof of the Exchange and other strategic positions around the town.

Local gunsmiths, John Parr, James Grady, Jonas Beakill, Croft Williamson, Richard Gildart Jnr. and Mr. Farmer were just some who regularly cleaned and maintained the town's muskets kept at the Tower in Water Street.

Also at the Tower a basement room known as Leather Hall was utilised as a guard room for soldiers, and a shop near the Exchange was established as a guard house for constables on watch duty.

In October, a detachment of troops from Lowthers regiment stationed in the south of England called at Chester and then marched into town. The unit consisted of a subaltern and 50 men and their purpose was to embark on the vessel HMS Looe* (newly built at the port) to guard the gunpowder that had been taken aboard from the towns' magazine.

Also anchored mid-river was the man-of-war "South Sea Castle"* and later "The Mercury"*. These vessels acted as a sea defence for the port and also monitored the ferrying of goods and people crossing the river for the safety of the Wirral. All surplus boats and ferries from within the area, had been tied together within gun range of the warships, ensuring they could not be utilised by enemy forces.

---

*HMS Looe - 5th rate man o'war 44 guns, 716 tons, 220-280 men. From Gorell and Parkes' yard, launched 17th August 1745.

*HMS South Sea Castle - 5th rate man o'war 44 guns, 712 tons, 220-280 men. From John O'Kills yard, launched 18th August 1745. John Amherst - Captain.

*HMS Mercury - 5th rate man o'war 24 guns, 504 tons, 140-160 men. From Richard Golightly's yard, launched 13th October 1745. William Bladewell - Captain.

Meanwhile fresh volunteers were still coming forward to sign for the regiment.

The amount of pay the soldiers would receive stood at a shilling (5p) a day to a private soldier and an additional 4d a day if they spent the time out of town (this pay was more than that received by many regular soldiers in His Majesty's regiments), and of course the pay of officers would be more than double this amount and proportionate to rank. The subscription money raised by the people of Liverpool had now increased to £4,859. This money was for the uniforms, equipment and the pay for the soldiers. The Corporation was able to purchase drums (from William Houlcroft), standards for their colours and a pair of ensigns. The style and colour of their uniform had been agreed upon and orders placed on 5th October stated their requirements "in a fortnight's time". They would have blue coats (the regular army, of course, wore red). These blue coats would be turned up with red (3,000 yards of kersey being ordered) at the front and the coats were fastened with white metal buttons. They would have black felt hats (52 dozen were ordered) which would be bound with white galloon; it was probable that they wore their own shirts and breeches, but they were provided with white stockings and black marching shoes.

The Officers would basically wear the same uniform, though with more elaborations in keeping with the normal 18th century practice.

Thirteen shoemakers in the town were already preparing 626 pairs of shoes at 4/2d per pair and 50 dozen strong white stockings had been ordered from Wales.

The following tradesmen were now frantically working "all out" so that the uniforms would be ready as soon as possible. These were:-

TAILORS

John Roberts	Richard Woolfall
John Barker	Edward Coppell
Thomas Naylor	Edward Howard
Robert Francis	Edward Roberts
Isaac Harrison	Thomas Dale
Mr. Carr	......Golding
John Brookes	Nathan Farrer
William Pennington	Robert Abraham

| James Kenyon | Jacob Jackson |
| James Lund | Edward Cropper |

HATTERS	**LACEMAKERS**
Richard Williams	Mrs. Sherwan
Thomas Fletcher	Mrs. Gregson
Samual Thomas	Mrs. Wilcock

STOCKINGS (FINISHERS)

| Edward Burrows | Mrs. Tatlock |

Whilst these uniforms were in the process of being prepared, The Liverpool Blues spent their early days drilling in their civilian clothes.

Volunteer Walter Shairpe began his account by writing about the new regiment:

"It was raised to defend the nation against the attempts made by the son of the Chevalier de St. George in the highlands of Scotland by the Corporation and inhabitants of Liverpool, upon subscriptions, which were begun to be taken on about the 1st of October 1745......and the commissions were granted to the officers who were to command it on the 4th of October, and again the 10th and 11th.

"There were officers and men for six companys, amongst which I was made a Lieutenant. Ever after that time we were imployed in disciplining the soldiers by their different companys, upon which they made very great progress, and now and then lining the street in honour of the Mayor and Corporation upon any Public days, which was all that was done worth notice, except our continually enlisting and discharging our men at the pleasure of the Corporation who were excessively unsteady in their re-solutions until the 10th November."

The novelty and enthusiasm eventually began to wear thin for the volunteers as 4 weeks passed with the rigmarole of repetitive muster parades, guard duties and foot drills, the various

A List of the Officers who
Comanded the light Company
of Liverpool Blues

Coll Graham & Coll Gordon &
Major Bendish Field Officers

1. Capt. Tongue Lieut. Whittle En Clacherog
2. Spencer Shairp Halsall
3. Mason Dunbar Kenyon
4. Stewart Strong Smith
5. Campbell Halliday Lee
6. Wrahly Armitage Strong
7. Heywood Heyes Todd
8. Colquitt Farmer Dugdale

Lieut. Dunbar Adjutant
Lieut. Whittle Quarter Maist.
Ens Lee Adjut. after Dunbar
threw it up at Wiggan

Another extact from Lt. Shairpe's account

28

Corporation officials all attempting to assist, but not entirely sure just how to administer the new regiment. With the commissions granted, the captains, lieutenants and ensigns now appointed, joined the ex-officers and disbanded NCO's who had previously seen service in His Majesty's army. All had taken the Oath of Loyalty to the King and had the Articles of War read to them. Every man was prepared to march at an hour's notice.

By the 10th November Shairpe was relieved to relate:

> "Colonel Graham and Colonel Gordon, two pritty gentlemen and very good soldiers, came down to command the regiment by his Majesty's order, and to our great happiness and joy at being no longer under the direction of a parcell of ignorent Aldermen."

These two field officers who would be joined later by a third, were first class soldiers; the officer who would take overall charge was Colonel William Graham.

Graham, born at Balliheridon, Co. Armagh, was a seasoned veteran of about 57 years of age. He had been appointed Ensign in Colonel Kirk's Regiment of Foot in 1706 and taken prisoner at Almanza in 1707, served with General Hills expedition to Canada in 1711, promoted to Lieut. Colonel of the Queens Regiment in 1723 and promoted to Colonel of the 43rd Light Infantry Regiment in 1741. The Corporation would bestow on him the rank of Brigadier Colonel.

Like all officers of the day, Colonel Graham had his servants and these had been instructed to march north from the south of England (as reinforcements) to join him. When they arrived they would act as "out riders" and messengers for the regiment once they had left town.

The second officer, Lieut. Colonel Alexander Gordon was another "no-nonsense" soldier, who had been a major in MacCartneys Scots Regiment in1710 and became a Lieut. Colonel in Colonel Fieldings Regiment in 1721.

On Monday 11th November, the 2 field officers ordered all companies on parade at daylight. There, the newly delivered arms from the Tower (of London) were handed out to the volunteers from 15 chests which had been delivered to the townfield*.

The companies were inspected by the Colonel who decided that there were 500 men up to standard, before rearranging, to reduce the number of men in each from 100 to 70 (excluding officers). He then created another company and appointed his nephew, 23 year old Ben Heywood, as Captain of this 7th company.

That day an express arrived in town with the news that the invading Scots had, in fact, crossed the border at 11 o'clock the previous morning and were marching south - in England.

Colonel Graham called for a meeting with the towns dignatories at the Mayor's house. This influential group represented the various important parties in the town; military, civic, merchants, shipowners and the church.**

After the meeting, Colonel Graham was far from happy with the outcome, but kept his opinions to himself and wrote the following letter to the War Office.

Liverpoole, 11th November 1745
9 o'clok at night

"My Lord,
"I take the liberty to acquaint your Lordship what occured here yesterday, and this day. Had the seven companies out,consisting of about five hundred as good men as could be expected, and delivered them the arms sent from the Tower.

---

*This traditional musket was an 11lb weapon with a 3ft barrel. It was not particularly accurate,relying more on fire power (rank by rank discharge). It had been with the army for 40 years and was termed affectionately "The Brown Bess".

**The meeting was attended by Col. Graham, Lt. Col. Gordon, James Broomfield, Owen Pritchard,Foster Cuncliffe, Charles Gore, Richard Kelsall, James Gildart, Edward Trafford, John Colquitt, John Hardman, William Carr, Samuel Ogden, Arthur Heywood, Edward Forbes, and Rev. Stanley.

"The Mayor of this Town had an express this day of the rebels passing the Eden yesterday morning at eleven and marched southward. Upon which I desired a consultation with the Mayor and such, and here enclose their expectations, which I shall follow to the best of my judgement.

"This town having no sort of defence but the houses. This is all I am able to acquaint your Lordship at present. ‾

I am, with great respect
Your Lordships most obedient,
humble servant
W. Graham"

A letter from the Corporation was enclosed with his, it read:

"It is thought adviseable that Mr. Mayor shall give directions to secure the Avenues of the Town, having received information that the rebels have passed the River Eden the 10th inst.

"It is recommended that Colonel Graham stay with the Liverpool Regiment of seven companies in Town untill he is ordered other ways by his superior officers.

"It is also agreed that when Colonel Graham can do no further service for the defence of the Town, he shall dispose of the force under his command as he shall judge best for his Majesty's service."

The dignatories of the town had again changed their minds (perhaps under the threat of the rebels actually on English soil) and their prime concern was again the defence of the town itself.

On the 12th November, Shairpe was writing:

...The 12th, nothing extaordinary happened, only this morn, hatts, shoes and stockings were delivered to them.

"The 13th, he (Col. Graham) reviewed them and put

them though the Manuall exercise and firing, with which he was greatly pleased, and gave a very good character of the officers."

By the 14th November the decision reached at the meeting by the civic dignatories on the 11th November now became common knowledge, creating a great discontent amongst the whole of the regiment. The soldiers were of the opinion that they would be joining the King's army as a regiment or combining with a volunteer or militia group, certainly making a more positive contribution to deal with the emergency. Shairpe voiced the feelings of his fellow officers, writing:

"...The 14th, nothing was done with the regiment, but a solution was made by this wise Corporation sáying we should lye in town to defend it against the enemy, which was so ridiculous a scheme that it had like to have put an end to the whole, as Colonel Graham was so much displeased at the town offering to force him into such a command and refusing to let him have the sole management of the men, that he had like to have left them altogether, and all the officers were determined to lay down their commissions if they had not leave to march, wherever the Colonel thought proper, as it was with that view that they had all entered into the scheme and not to defend the town in particular. However, upon second thoughts they gave that up and left the whole to the Colonel."

With feelings running high in the "Blues", more meetings took place and it was finally decided that for the good of the common cause the regiment should march out of town and join up with the army of the Duke of Cumberland, whose troops were now massing somewhere in the south of England.

Another battalion was now formed to defend the town itself, consisting of 5 companies of 70 men each officered by tradesmen and other respected members of the community.

The two officers chosen were Captain White and Captain Pole. This regiment would be self-supporting (receiving no pay),. although the corporation did make a concession to cover minor expenses, refreshments and provide beer etc.

This new battalion of volunteers would act solely as a "Home Guard" with nightly patrols on a rota basis and they would assist the constables of the town supplementing the "watch" and keeping order.

On the morning of Friday 15th November the soldiers were finally "kitted out" having now received their new blue coats and the last of their accoutrements.

They were ready to march. The drummers had been beating throughout the early morning as last minute preparations were made; the gathering crowds of families and friends milling around the new force and wishing them well on their venture against the rebel army.

There was much back slapping and hand shaking and drink was passed about liberally through the ranks as the officers attempted to create some semblance of order; the NCO's organising those handling the baggage wagon which was packed with tents and all equipment that a marching army would require ensuring also the powder wagon's tarpaulin* was securely lashed into place to keep out the rain and damp over the coming weeks.

These "last minute preparations" dragged on into late afternoon, when the drummers finally "beat-up" for "on parade". The ensigns unfurled their new regimental standards and the colours caught and fluttered in the afternoon breeze encouraging more cheers from the enthusiastic crowd. The mounted officers wheeled their charges into line and the NCO's positioned their various companies into a "dressed in" formation; muskets were brought up into marching order throughout the ranks. The Colonel indicated that all was ready and the NCO's barked out the orders to commence marching; and with the drummers "beating" out their incessant parradiddle rhythm, the soldiers headed out of town up the London road towards Prescot. The crowds still cheering and singing as the baggage wagons pulled in to the rear, their highwheels lurching along the rutted highway. To the left of the marching men, creaking and turning in the soft evening breeze, were "The Gallows Mills"standing like grim monuments over the spot where the gibbets had supported the corpses of the previous rising 30 years earlier and testament to Liverpool's last involvement against a rebel force.

Within an hour the beat of the drums was fading into the distance and with dusk approaching rapidly, the well wishers began drifting back into town. The Liverpool Blues would spend their first night away from home at Prescot.

---

*New tarpaulin sheet supplied by Miles Towson

CHAPTER III

On the 9th of November up on the northern border about 5,000 Highlanders accompanied by their camp followers, wives, doxies and the general riff-raff that followed 18th century armies, had poured across the River Eden to the incessant rant of their war pipes, the shrill tones driving them onwards at their usual rapid pace, now even more eager that they were on English soil.

This army on the march covered an area in distance of 7 miles, separated into 2 divisions, with usually half a day's march between them. This was purely to facilitate accommodation for the 2 groups as the majority of towns at that time was very small, offering limited shelter.

A great many of these Highlanders were young men, some mere boys, who had been practically dragged from their small crofts and homesteads. Others were herdsmen taken from their flocks and, to say the least, reluctant followers; but the backbone of the Scots army, the experienced soldier, was a ferocious adversary. These wild fighting men were described in a contemporary report thus "...the majority of them seemed of a strong active and hardy warrior, whose average build was set off by their Highland dress to advantage, their stern countenances and bushy uncombed hair with bonnet pulled low over their faces gave them a fierce and barbarous and imposing aspect", they spoke in the Irish gaelic which was alien even to Lowland Scots. These fearsome mountain men were the Macdonalds, the Macgregors, the Camerons, McKenzies, Gordons and Macintosh, each man armed with a miscellaneous array of weaponry: broad swords and firelocks, dirks and targes. "A 100 or so were armed with scythe blades attached to pitchfork shafts." These were the Macgregors whose frantic swinging blades could cut the legs from a running charger or decapitate a horse soldier through the middle at a full gallop.

The Highlanders' broadsword could make any battlefield a spectacle of horror being covered with severed heads, legs and arms and mutilated bodies, the battle at Prestonpans which had taken place just 20 days earlier (21st September) was no exception.

Riding before this Highland horde, the express riders would carry the stories to the towns of Lancashire of the barbaric battles taking place in the north. The people there would pass on the news by word of mouth and the brutalities became atrocities and these became even more exaggerated in the telling with the Highlanders, finally being accused of cannabalism. The news of course creating panic in towns and villages with the more wealthy evacuating their families and goods to safer areas.

One of Prince Charles's advisers was a Lord George Murray, probably the most outstanding of all his aides and perhaps, if Charles had heeded the advice of this man instead of being at loggerheads and bickering with him, history may well have told a different story.

Murray had Liverpool connections. His Grandmother was a Stanley and his father had been born at Knowsley. He was familiar with the "lye of the land" in Lancashire and had a good instinct for making the correct moves. He was a political animal and a brilliant military strategist. It was he who had organised the Highland army, out-manoeuvering General Wade, the English Commander (positioned then at Newcastle-upon-Tyne) and was able to slip past him over the border to finally encircle Carlisle.

Murray appeared to foresee and appreciate many situations before they arose and in the coming months he would be proved right time and time again.

At the time the rebels were surrounding Carlisle, the concerned Lord Derby at Knowsley Hall was still struggling in his attempts to organise the county militia. He wrote to the Duke of Newcastle at the War Office lamenting the lack of cooperation by the gentlemen of the county, many of them still bickering over subscription money and a lack of experienced officers within their catchment area. It was proposed to give the militia men a 1/- a day in an endeavour to encourage more volunteers, "but this may create discontentment" he reflected "amongst the King's troops as the militia were so inferior to them". He was also concerned over clothing "a uniform appears necessary, and yet if it be paid for out of the private subscription, a much less number of men must be raised". He was in a quandry - should the county pay this substantial rate? (A professional soldier could expect 6d a day with reductions.) His Lordship had to decide whether to achieve the quota of men required or reduce their pay and have decent and respectable uniforms.

Lord Derby's letter also mentioned the large number of popish gentry in Lancashire as a reason for the lack of support and brought the War Secretary's attention to the fact that "Liverpool had taken £5,000 from us with their separate scheme".

Over in Chester, Lord Derby's counterpart Lord Cholmondeley, had similar problems with his county militia but the Lords of that county were able to raise their own volunteer groups privately from their estates and tied tenants, amongst them were the Cheshire and Staffordshire Militia. Lord Herbert's new regiment and 600 county militia men swelled the numbers.

Cholmondeley appears to have had more success and co-operation regarding the organisation of his forces having raised the county militia plus a nobleman's militia.

The loyalist Lords of the county rallied around for the defence of the city of Chester profoundly aware of its strategic position as the gateway into North Wales.

The castle there was considered a likely target by the oncoming rebels. They could march through Lancashire, cross the Mersey at Warrington, veer west into Wales and there link up with the powerful border and Welsh families like the Wynns and the Wyndhams. Both families were considered loyal to the Jacobite cause and could raise many of the populace whose sympathies lay with the Stuarts.

Most roads into North Wales led through the old fortified garrison town of Chester and Cholmondeley's superiors had instructed him to defend the position "to the last extremity". He accordingly set about the mammoth task of repairing and securing the fortress that had long fallen in many places to a state of disrepair.

He employed 700 men, the majority of them soldiers, but there were also carpenters, bricklayers, masons and paviours, all assisting under the administration of Field Officers and a Military Engineer, Alexander de Lavaux, to bring the fortifications of the town to a standard that could withstand a siege.

The ditches of the castle were deepened and new trenches dug. Carters were employed, carrying timber from the surrounding forests for stockades to reinforce the weaker portions of the walls, platforms were erected and stonework dressed for making up the gates. Empty casks, wool packs and sandbags were organised to cover the magazine as a shelter. Covered walkways and gangways were constructed behind the walls to facilitate quick movement from one area to another. All the preparations necessary to repel the rebels, should they appear, was organised with great urgency, although his Lordship was not at all optimistic of resistance should the rebels arrive with cannon.

Lord Cholmondeley also appears to have paid the greater part of the expenses out of his own pocket, but naturally kept stringent accounts of the expenses of the enterprise and made continuous reminders of the fact in his correspondence to the War Office (in case they overlooked his generosity after the cessation of the emergency).

His organisation appears to have been very thorough, calling for the examination of the cannon held at the castle (eighteen in all) and found both ordinance, stores and guns defective and in short supply.

Cholmondeley was forced to send to Liverpool for a number of large cannon and stores to accompany them.

From the "men of war" anchored in Liverpool he also acquired swivel guns (1 pounders) and shot to match. These light guns could easily be manhandled from one position to another, on and along the Chester walls, although he himself doubted whether a prolonged siege could be maintained as the walls encompassed a 2 mile circumference and still had many weak positions.

Also from Liverpool he recruited 36 sailors, 20 of them Warrant Officers from the large privateers or guinea men and all experienced gunners.

Photo-F. Simpson, F.S.A.

Chester Castle

Lord Cholmondeley had been instructed to defend the position "to the last extremity".

He organised mattrosses* and had them working 16 hours out of 24, filling shells, making up cartridges and grapeshot, packing the hand grenades and cohorns** but consenting them double pay for their labours.

Over in Lancashire his counterpart, the Lord Lieutenant of the county, was having less success. Situated in a direct line with the oncoming invaders he was still in the throes of sorting through the legalities and petty squabbles of his Deputy Lieutenants, attempting to institute some kind of organisation of the county militia. Finally, it was ordered to muster the Lancashire militia on the 14th November with only 14 days pay.

The county parishers immediately began sending their quota of men for the militia service.

In Sefton the "Muster-Master" set about organising and preparing the villages of that parish for the onslaught of the rebels, the constable there having journeyed to Liverpool to collect arms and accoutrements, currently being maintained by the gunsmiths of the port. The constable had searched the catholic homesteads in the area for horses and arms, his duties also included escorting the men up to Ormskirk to be enrolled in the county militia regiments.

In other parishes and towns in the area the story would be the same as at Bickerstaffe. The constables there reported that "time and money was spent searching for men to impress into service" which would be accordingly costed against the parish.

The sole aim of these volunteers was "to be ready to give the little assistance in our power to Marshall Wade" when he arrived.

Unfortunately, Marshall Wade had no intention of marching his army across the Pennines to intercept the Scots in Lancashire. He had been outwitted by Lord George Murray into sitting tight at Newcastle-on-Tyne. Consequently, the rebels were able to slip virtually unopposed into Lancashire.

---

*Mattrosses - assisted the gunners in traversing, sponging, loading and firing guns.
**Cohorn - a mortar of $4\,^2/_5$ inches calibre. Named after Coehorn, a Dutch military engineer

Wade wrote to Derby with the following:-

> "All the advice I can give you is that if you have any
> armed force, as most counties have, to make use of it,
> by dividing it into small parties, who may fire from
> every hedge and keep the rebels from separating from
> the main body (to) pillage and plunder, which I think
> will embarass them more than any other method that
> can be expected from county regiments."

So Lord Derby's militia men could expect no assistance from Marshall Wade. There was no army in Lancashire to halt or impede the invaders, the military that had been in the county had departed. The Liverpool Blues had left the town on the 15th November and were now intending to march south to join Sir John Ligonier's army.

Lancashire had no defence whatsoever. Derby decided to move the militia headquarters from Bury and Chorley and march his force to Liverpool, if only to safeguard the muskets they had collected from the various parishes.

The "Blues" had left late on the Friday afternoon and to quote from Shairpe's account:-

> "... We got no further than Prescott that night, as it
> was late before we got out of the town, and most of
> the men got drunk by the generosity of their friends
> at parting..."

The following morning they marched to Warrington and acquired good quarters throughout the town where they stayed for 3 days "without anything extraordinary happening".

On the Wednesday of the 20th November at 2 o'clock in the morning an express rider rode in with the news that the enemy would now have arrived at Kendal (actually they did not enter the town until the 22nd November) nevertheless, they were marching through the Northern counties at an alarming speed.

By 6 a.m. the "Blues" drummers were beating "to arms" and the companies "fell in" for muster parade at the Corn Market. They marched out of town at 8 a.m. across the Warrington bridge and out of Lancashire into the County of Cheshire.

Many volunteer groups would not travel beyond their county boundaries but the Liverpool Blues did not consider any such restrictions.

After crossing the Mersey they headed south; 6 of the companies going to Northwich about 8 miles away and Captain Campbell with his 5th company, splitting from the regiment and taking all the baggage to Stone via Newcastle-under-Lyme. All companies marching south intended to join the English armies massing there.

The next day the 6 companies lay at Northwich and Col. Graham and Captain Heywood went to Nantwich expecting to meet some of the general officers in an endeavour to join the main body of the army. They found no military there, but did receive a message from a Sir William Young with orders to return to Warrington.

Sir John Ligonier in the South had received his orders to "make himself master of the Mersey". In turn, Col. Graham received his, addressed to "Officer, Commander-in-Chief, Regiment of Volunteers raised for His Majesty's service in Liverpool", dated 19th November. They read:-

> "It is His Majesty's pleasure that you continue with the regiment under your command at Warrington, and that you do, according to your judgement and discretion endeavour to secure and fortify the bridges there and thereabouts and use all other endeavours in obstructing the rebels in case they should attempt to march southwards, for which purpose more troops will join you as soon as possible. But in case any great body of the rebels should approach you so near as to make it impractical for you to defend the pass and no further assistance should be arrived, you are to retire to Chester, in all which you are to act according to the best of your judgement; and to obey such orders as you shall receive from Sir John Ligonier or other your superior officer, and if you shall have left Warrington before this comes to your hands you are forthwith to return hither and put in execution the orders aforesaid."

That evening Lieut. Farmer came into Northwich with Captain Colquitt's No. 8 Company, which had only been raised after the other 7 had left for Warrington.

A story told about the Liverpool Blues after the cessation of the war, and in all probability Colquitt's company, relates how after leaving Liverpool and before the company arrived at Warrington, the weary soldiers in the half light of dusk had struggled onto Penketh Common: -

> "Suddenly the ears of the tired men were pierced with horrid shrieks and dismal screams, issuing from the depths of the darkness. The command was given to halt and form close column, the scouts were sent in advance with instructions to observe all caution. In their absence the suspense increased their agony as the shrieks continued.
>
> "The scouts returned and how great the change, they reported a large flock of geese undertaking a mass migration, the dark moorland became the scene of scrambling soldiers all attempting to capture the 'enemy'. The company arrived in Warrington each man with a goose under his arm where they enjoyed a goodly supper on the cold November night."

This would be told in later years around the firesides of Liverpool and jokingly referred to as the first "victory" of the Liverpool Blues.

The next morning the companies marched from Northwich back to Warrington setting off about 9 a.m. and arriving about noon, were their orders were confirmed regarding the defence of the bridge.

That night Captain Campbell rode in with his 5th Company and with fresh horses, unfortunately, the baggage had been left at Newcastle which meant the soldiers had only the clothes they stood up in.

Next day Ensign Todd of the 7th Company returned to retrieve it.

All that day, 23rd November, the "Blues" positioned themselves about the bridge and Brigadier Douglas arrived from Chester to assess the situation and consult with Col. Graham regarding the defence of that position. Later in the day they dined with Mr. Blackburn of Orford, the Brigadier returning to Chester in the evening.

After the departure of the Brigadier another visitor arrived to join the "Blues". He was Major Richard Bendish. He was the 3rd Officer of the line to join the regiment.

Major Bendish was of course another member of the landed gentry, born in 1700 in Cambridgeshire. The Major had a reputation as a "hot head", but again he was an experienced officer, his commission having been renewed in 1727 and appointed Major of the 7th Marines just 6 months earlier. He had applied for transfer to the "Blues" upon hearing of their formation. The Liverpool regiment was now complete.

The following morning, Col. Graham received orders by an express rider from Chester Castle to now pull down the Warrington bridge.

Lord Cholmondely, Brigadier Douglas and the field officers of the several regiments in the garrison at Chester had decided that, in the absence of troops in the county of Lancashire, the only way to obstruct the advance of the rebels was to destroy all access across the River Mersey.

The orders Col. Graham had received upon being aroused from his bed were the following:

24th November

"Sir

I wrote to you immediately on the return of Brigadier General Douglas who has been over by the Duke's (of Cumberland) order to view the Bridge at Warrington to see if it was practicable to make a Tete-de-Pont in order to secure and defend the same, as being a very material pass. And as the making of one is found impracticable it is the unanimous opinon of the Brigadier and all the Field Officers, as well as my own, that no time is to be lost in breaking down the same. I therefore write this, by express, with my positive orders to see the same effected, to which end you will get what assistance of workmen the town will afford, and the proper utensils that it may be done out of hand. It is not my intention that the bridge should be entirely ruined, but only the two middle arches taken entirely down, and especially the middle pier, which must be taken down level with the water.

"This will effectively prevent the rebels being able to make any passage and yet leave the repair of it very practicable and at an easy expense at a proper season of the year When this work is executed you will immediately comply with your orders from Brigadier William Young, who I think directs you to Chester, without you receive any orders to the contrary from Sir John Ligonier or your superior officers.

I remain (with great sincerity)
Your most obedient humble servant
Cholmondeley

These orders by express were received at 2 a.m. and by 5 a.m. 10 men from each company had begun the task of taking down the old bridge.

Throughout the day locally hired labour was brought in to assist the Liverpool men. The bridge was a solid structure, consisting of four stone arches and it was not until 8 p.m. that the two centre

(*Warrington Library*)

Warrington Bridge
Rebuilt 1746 the original demolished
to the water level 1745.

arches were down, and the central support to water level. The regiment had now withdrawn to the Cheshire side of the river, the soldiers now being accommodated over a large area in the surrounding villages, the billetting there being less satisfactory in the small homesteads and farms south of the river, although Shairpe does comment that he was fortunate to get good quarters "at a Mr. Hall's, a little country squire with two pritty daughters".

The next morning Lt. Shairpe was sent as quartermaster to Frodsham where he met Col. Graham and Brigadier Douglas coming from Chester to Latchford.

The orders for the day were for Captains Tongue and Heywoods' companies to guard the bridge and a breast work raised upon the end of it, the other companies cantooned in Frodsham then mounted guard throughout the night.

News arrived regularly by express, the latest rider reporting to them that the rebels had now advanced and were as near as Preston where there had been no opposition in Lancashire to them. In fact, with the Scots at Preston and the English army still organising themselves in the Midlands and the South, the Liverpool Blues encamped upon the banks of the Mersey were now positioned between the two opposing factions the only troops apparently involved in the exercise of actually attempting to impede the progress of the rebels.

But it was the kind of work that a militia group could have undertaken and Col. Graham appears to have made known his views to Lord Cholmondeley and his dissatisfaction at the orders continually splitting up his regiment into companies and acting as working parties. It was not in keeping with his view of an infantry regiment as he considered his "Blues".

By now the Duke of Cumberland had received the news at his HQ in the south of the demolition of the Warrington Bridge and sent orders to Cholmondeley "to prevent by all possible means the rebels from crossing the Mersey".

These detailed orders called for the breaking down of all the bridges. Of course, it would be difficult stopping foot soldiers crossing the river upstream near Manchester. There, many places were reasonably fordable (especially at low tide), but the lack of constructed crossing places could seriously affect the progress of the thirty one baggage wagons and carts, many of which were drawn by 2 and 3 horses, plus the 12 artillery pieces that were essential to the rapid moving army.

Accordingly, Cholmondeley sent his orders to the Liverpool Blues via Brigadier Douglas: to destroy all the crossing points between Warrington and Stockport Bridge. This meant any ferries as well as bridges, plus any fording positions.

South of Salford the 2 rivers, the Mersey and the Irwell, ran across country east to west representing a natural twin barrier to an army advancing from the north.

On the Mersey, between the towns of Warrington and Stockport, there were 3 bridges and 3 main ferry points. On the Irwell there were 2 bridges and a ferry. All would receive the attention of the "Blues".

Cholmondely directed that the bridge linking Salford and Manchester, "The Salford Bridge" be destroyed but this bridge in fact survived: perhaps it was too well guarded by Jacobite sympathizers or the "Blues" were unable to reach the position in time. Cholmondely also gave orders to take the ferries on the Mersey down to the broad waters at Liverpool and anchor them mid river, but those on the Irwell were to be sunk, and "the banks of the rivers were to be destroyed" to prevent the construction of temporary bridges "and altered so as to render the river impassible".

A remark in the orders given to Brigadier Douglas however, illustrates a disagreement that was beginning to emerge between Cholmondely and Colonel Graham. He continues:

> "... I have no temptation to leave it to the conduct and execution of Col. Graham, considering what has already happened upon so many occasions and I flatter myself you will excuse me in taking the liberty to desire to execute my orders."

On Tuesday the 26th November at about 7 a.m. the drummer beat "to arms" and between 9 a.m. and 10 a.m. the "Blues" set out under the command of Brigadier Douglas to destroy the bridges. Captain Colquitt's company went to Latchford to relieve Col. Graham and the 2 companies guarding that position.

As Colquitt's company stayed to hold Warrington bridge, the 1st and 7th Company under Col. Gordon then set out for the River Irwell.

The remaining 5 companies with Col. Graham and Major Bendish marched to Stockport; Lt. Shairpe estimated it as "21 computed miles". It was not a straight journey as en-route they stopped at Altringham, where they empressed carters, their horses, masons and carpenters, 16 men in all, that would assist in the breaking down of the Stockport Bridge.

They arrived late at Stockport, carrying tools that had been acquired on the journey, each man exhausted, especially Lt. Shairpe who had been commanding the rear which finally arrived in the town at 1 o'clock in the morning.

At 5 a.m. the same morning, Col. Graham had his men up again to the beat of the drums, the soldiers reluctantly dragging themselves from their beds with the Col. threatening to put the officers under arrest for not appearing on parade as promptly as himself.

After much complaining the fatigued officers managed to get the equally exhausted men started on the work of dismantling the bridge. Ten men were delegated from each company, plus the impressed men from Altringham.

By the end of the day the bridge was down. A letter from a Stockport inhabitant confirms:-

"We are in the utmost confusion here, all the bridges on the Mersey being ordered to be destroyed. That at Warrington was demolished on Sunday and that at Barton last night, a party of 500 of the Liverpool Blues marched into town with orders to destroy the bridge here."

Next day, the Brigadier gave orders about 10 a.m. for the companies of Captain Spencer and Captain Mason to proceed to Crossford where another stone bridge linking Stretford and Altringham straddled the river. This was about 6 miles from Stockport.

They arrived at 11 o'clock. Lieut. Shairpe wrote:

> "At noon we began that piece of work which our
> men were now getting very alert at, and fond of, as it
> was mischief. However, the bridge was well built
> and our tools were so blunted that it stood until 6
> next morning (28th November), although it had but
> one arch. Then we received an order from the
> Brigadier and Col. Graham, who lay that night at
> Altringham, to leave off working, which was done
> accordingly, but it was so far cut down that the whole
> bridge fell in half an hour after we left it."

Whilst the 2nd and 4th companies were pulling down the bridge
at Crossford, Col Gordon with the 1st and 7th companies were at
Barton (near Eccles) destroying the stone bridge, crossing the River
Irwell. They also destroyed a wooden bridge at Hulme and sank
all the boats including the Irlam Ferry.

In the exercise, the wooden bridge at Carrington was also
destroyed and the Hollin Ferry met the same fate as the one at
Irlam. The river banks at fordable positions were destroyed or
damaged and the course of the waterways in some places diverted.
Some of the regiment then made their way back to Latchford
leaving behind one of their colleagues, a William Liversley, who,
probably sick, died and was buried at Cheadle churchyard on
December 4th. Arriving back at Latchford they continued to
Frodsham and destroyed the bridge crossing the River Weaver.
The exercise was complete. Every crossing point from Warrington
to Stockport had been destroyed, there were now no roads out of
South Lancashire.

This dismantling of the bridges would not actually stop the Scots
army but it could hinder and divert them and cause reorganisation
certainly regarding their baggage wagons and artillery. In the main,
it would give the army in the Midlands valuable time with their
mustering of troops and hopefully allowing them to "close in".
At Preston, Prince Charles and his Jacobite forces had arrived on
27th November, allowing his army a full day's rest, primarily
with a view to encourage recruitment and to assess his position to
date.

Throughout his enforced march through England Charles had
advocated tact and diplomacy and his soldiers in general

throughout the campaign to date refrained from looting and disturbance. He endeavoured to encourage volunteers to his ranks with the slogan "Church and Liberty" and the promise of a new system in society, reflected by his disciplined army. The use of force against civilians was condemned; actually there was little plundering of the populace. Food, horses and wagons were exchanged for I.O.U.'s with the promise of payment after the overthrow of the Hanoverians. What he did confiscate was crown monies, bonds etc. These, he considered, would be his eventually anyway. He had envisaged Preston, if not exactly a rallying point for loyal Jacobites, at least as a focal point for English recruits to swell and enhance his Scots army. This was mainly Jacobite country and the future success of how his campaign may fare would be indicated by the amount of volunteers flocking to follow his flag.

Charles had told his council of war at Carlisle that he was in possession of letters from his friends who would rise to join him, upon his arrival in England. His reception in Preston was quite favourable with church bells ringing and cheering crowds on the streets to welcome the Highland men as they poured into the town.

When the proclaimation had been read (declaring the father of Prince Charles as King), there were loud hurrahs from the townspeople, but he must have still felt ill at ease.

There were many Catholic gentlemen about the town who ensured that the Prince and his army were comfortably billetted for the night in the locality and there could certainly be no complaints about the hospitality of the people, but there were murmurings among the Highland men. The town itself gave the superstitious clansmen a sense of foreboding. It was here that the 1715 Rebellion had come to an end and many had misgivings about getting beyond Preston, just wishing to get the place behind them.

Lord George Murray took the initiative and gathered together a number of the Highlanders and crossed the River Ribble and quartering his men on the south side of the town in a bid to dispel any illusions the men may have had. Preston was the first town in England that gave the Prince some indication of assistance and Charles Edward must have breathed a somewhat sigh of relief that here at last some support was joining his ranks.

Amongst the assortment of volunteers who came forward to join his army was Francis Towneley, a gentleman of distinction. He was the 5th son of Charles Towneley of Towneley in Lancashire.

Like his father, he was a keen Jacobite and at 23 he had joined the French army holding a commission and distinguishing himself with his courage and conduct on the battlefields of Europe; at the outbreak of the rebellion, living amongst friendly Jacobites in Wales, he had received a Colonel's commission from the King of France to raise forces for the Stuart cause. He joined the Prince at Preston, confident he could encourage many supporters of his home county to join him. Francis Towneley would prove to be a zealous follower of the young Prince, a man prepared to die for his beliefs and considered that his fellow men should at least feel the same.

The Council held by Charles and his chiefs must have been more than a little subdued. Preston had shown enthusiasm and support but nothing like the mass of recruits had come forward as the Prince had promised to all and sundry.

After the seizure of public monies they still observed a code of good conduct as they proceeded out of town. This "No Provocation" order stood them in good stead as there was not even any minor skirmishes en route to hinder their advance. But it was no use marching for Warrington. Reports had now reached Charles regarding the destruction of the bridge and removal of the ferries, although, perhaps he had never really intended the Warrington route in the first place. His War Council may have kept an open mind deciding policy as events unfolded, although earlier Lord George Murray had advocated a "call" on Liverpool to collect a "contribution" suggesting Warrington was probably intended as the original route.

The Prince now insisted to his aides that many would join him from the Manchester area. They rested overnight at Preston and marched out the following morning on the road to Wigan and Manchester.

Liverpool, was witnessing a general state of alarm as the invading army loomed ever closer. Captain Colquitt of the "Blues" had in his civilian capacity as Customs Control Officer for the port, written in September to the Crown Authorities (after first forwarding his cash collections by post):-

> "I humbly beg you'll please to give me your
> directions how I shall act for the best to secure his
> Majesty's monies and bonds that may be in my hands.
> I thank God at present I have no money, but the value

of the bonds is upwards of £90,000 which gives me
great uneasiness and therefore beg you will give me
your directions how I shall govern myself about such
an emergency."

"Mr. Colquitt had also taken the precaution of leaving his house
in Peter Street and evacuating his wife and children to the Cheshire
peninsula. It was a measure adopted by many families: some
individuals within the population were bordering on panic. One
Liverpool man wrote in a letter:-

"In the midst of a distraction not to be credited, I
have stolen a few minutes to write to you. You need
not be informed that over apprehension arises from
the rebels being so near to us. Our affairs are come to
crisis, for this place is too rich to expect escaping a
party for contribu tion or plunder, or perhaps both.

"There is scarce a woman stays in the town, all fly
to the other side of the river in Cheshire, where great
numbers have been this last fortnight, and their most
valuable effects are on board ships which lie under.
the cannon of 2 men of war lately built here, which
are now in the channel. On this occasion lodgings
are raised prodigiously in all the villages on the other
side of the water, that a single room will fetch 10/=
(50p) a week, nothing can equal the horrors and fright
of the people. All last night carts were taking goods
away, carpenters were also at work making boxes for
packing and all furniture is packed and moved. There
is hardly any goods left in town. In a word. Liverpool
is stripped almost entirely. The progress the rebels
make must give the most dreadful apprehensions to
what they may do to all friends of our happy
establishment."

The surrounding parishes were also in a furore. In the parish
church of Walton-on-the-Hill the church warden there would write
later of his "carrying and recarrying the church plate and his
troubles trying to hide the valuables of the church".

With the belief that the Scottish army would "visit" Liverpool, all the parishes adjacent to the port were, of course, in a crisis. There was no defence against the rebels, there was no military, no arms, in fact the Highlanders could literally "walk in" since most able bodied men were with the Lancashire militia which had been hurriedly organised at Bury and Chorley into some semblance of order. They were a rag-tag outfit, both their uniforms and weapons leaving a lot to be desired. In fact, much of the men's clothing was their own civilian clothes and their weapons were a miscellaneous assortment of old firearms which although maintained were mostly outdated having been stored in the parish of their enrolment for many years.

The militia men would have been no match for the ferocious Highland men and their professional officers. Nor were they meant to be. Their role was not so much military as policing, ensuring against riot and offering stability in the path of the oncoming Scots. The enemy could have been harrassed but Lord Derby and his fellow officers decided strongly against action of this nature. They were fully aware that the recruits were unprepared and untrained for that kind of venture.

Besides, they certainly could not risk losing the muskets in their possession to the enemy. Many of the weapons of the county were now held by the militia force at the Chorley and Bury headquarters. It was appreciated that the amalgamation of the Lancashire militia had come too late to conduct any positive action against the rebels who were now practically upon them. Their prime concern had to be the safeguarding of these firearms.

It was now decided, having finally assembled the county weaponry, that it would be best to deposit them for safe keeping at a place where they could be best utilised and that place was the nearest garrison at Chester. This move would prevent those weapons falling into the hands of the Jacobite soldiers.

The militia had enough money to mobilise and pay them for a fortnight only and it was considered prudent to use this time, and men, to escort the arms to Liverpool for shipment to Chester.

Accordingly it was decided to alter their headquarters from Bury and Chorley to the Port of Liverpool.

The militia set out, the detachment from Bury and 2 companies from Chorley, Lord Derby setting up his new headquarters at the Talbot Hotel in Water Street.

(Lv.R.O.)

Talbot Hotel

Headquarters for Lord Derby's Lancashire Militia from November 21st.

Some companies of the militia from the north of Lancashire appear to have stayed detached from the main body and took part in later events north of Preston.

The main body from Bury arrived in the town on the 21st November (those from Chorley on the 23rd) just 4 days before the rebels took Preston. One group passing through Aughton buried one of their colleagues there in the church yard, a John Taylor of Cartmel who was killed accidentally by a halbert.

Lord Derby and his officers met at their new headquarters in Water Street and were of the unanimous opinion that the militia would now have to be disbanded, the "red tape" deeming it illegal to pay the men for more than 14 days service.

This meeting also confirmed that "the arms of the militia be put aboard a vessel in the port and taken to Chester", but some were to be distributed to "private men to take home with them, promising to secure them from the rebels". More than likely these would be the volunteers of the independant companies set up when the "Blues" left town. These volunteers would now be armed; their duties to guard and protect property within the town and act as a police keeping force ready to deter any lawless elements within.

CHAPTER IV

Liverpool anticipated the "visit" of the rebel army by making final preparations for the defence of the town.

By now all the bonds, deeds and corporation accounts and treasures had been taken aboard the ships on the river where men-of-war kept a silent vigil, overlooking the river scene as small boats scurried to and fro across the water carrying the endless stream of evacuees to the Wirral.

These small boats, some with sail, some manned by oarsmen, many overladen with passengers and goods had to manoeuvre around the bobbing islands of small boats lashed together in mid-channel; these craft were an assortment of small ferries and flats from up river together with half constructed boats from the many yards on the shores. Row boats and merchantmen, anything that could float and be used by the rebels had been taken and tied up to buoys within range of the warships' guns.

Within the town, now stripped of all moveable items, particularly anything of value, the majority attempted to go about their business as normal as possible. The now armed independent companies assisting the town constables to keep order.

There was no pay for these volunteers but there were compensations by way of free ale for each duty, courtesy of the Corporation and obtained from the many beer shops* about the town.

Duties included a strict rota of guarding, patrols and cleaning and maintaining their fire-arms in the tower armoury at Water Street. Their responsibilities also meant keeping watch from the high vantage positions above the town. Any travellers from the north would be stopped and asked about their business and any "intelligence" was quickly conveyed to the apprehensive Corporation.

Most townsfolk were comparatively calm but there was a certain tension in the air, most people convinced the rebels would call and demand a contribution.

Suddenly news arrived that not only was the Highland army

---

* The Beer Shop keepers were Richard Grimshaw, Samuel Parr, Art Davies, Peter Hardus, Edward Eastham, Mrs. Parkes

advancing rapidly, but they had actually been spotted on the other side of Warbreck Moor. This was the bleak sweeping hollow of moorland between Walton-on-the-Hill and Melling Mount - just six miles north of the town.

A contemporary report relates:

> "Every man capable of holding a musket, with a spark of loyalty in his composition, turned out to meet and repel the enemy, wives and children clung around their husbands and parents on their departure, entreating them not to expose themselves to any unnecessary danger."
> "The crowd of volunteers gathering outside the Exchange were startled when a high civic functionary, not unmindful of the importance of his valuable life, ran towards the dock en-route to the Cheshire shore, exclaiming as he ran down Water Street `A boat! A boat!'"

The gallant patriots then marched in the opposite direction towards Walton.

On arriving at Warbreck Moor, the cause of all the alarm was a commotion of figures on the distant ridge - partly obscured by rising dust clouds - who in fact, were only yelling drovers driving their sheep herds, the blurr of the harmless invaders being mistaken for the approaching army.

William, Duke of Cumberland, was still busy mustering his armies about Litchfield and attempting to gather together some 12,000 soldiers, many of whom had been shipped over from the continent where the war was still in full progress. But he was forever mindful that should he turn his back on France, the French army might just follow his own.

He wrote to Liverpool on the 29th November from Litchfield.

"Gentlemen of the Magistracy of Liverpool. The proof of fidelity and zeal which you have given and give upon this important occasion and of which Col. Graham has made a very exact report, are, as they ought to be extremely agreeable to me; and I must earnestly recommend to you to pursue in the same laudable and honourable course and at the same time let you know how much it will be for the King's and the nation's service that you should not be induced either by entreaties or menaces to call back your boats and vessels of the kind soever which you have sent off and put under the protection of his Majesty's ships of war, but that you leave them there in the persuasion that the utmost care will be had of them and which by the messenger I recommend in the strongest manner to the commanding officer of these ships. I am very sorry your courage and good affections are put to so severe a trial and that you are exposed to so great inconvenience; but I hope the time of your deliverance draws nigh and that by the blessing of the almighty these insolent plunderers will soon receive the just reward of their villainies. This army will be formed in a day or two when I shall endeavour to pursue such courses as will most effectually contribute to that end. I cannot help taking notice to you how much pleasure the account Colonel Graham gives me of your regiment; be assured I shall do everything that may contribute to your ease and contentment and to give you the most effective marks of my esteem; and that I am truly

> Your good friend WILLIAM
> By His Royal Highness's Command
> Everard Fawkener (Secretary)

It appears that the merchants of Liverpool had managed to get an agent to infiltrate the rebel army, who came south through Lancashire with them, sending out intelligence reports and updates of information which he obtained and sent via Chester to the Duke of Cumberland.

On the 28th November the rebel army set out from Preston to Manchester.

Lord George Murray, still seeking to march via Liverpool to collect a levy from the town was thwarted by a thumbs down from Prince Charles's war council. The decision now was to make all haste for Manchester. Consequently, they marched to Wigan passing within 15 miles of Liverpool collecting a few recruits en route at Burnley. However, a surveillance party was detoured to observe the position at Warrington and to check out all options for crossing the river. The advance party of Scots arrived in Manchester.

Lt. Shairpe writes:

> "This morning, the 28th (Thursday), Colonel
> Graham set out to seek the Duke of Cumberland at

Litchfield, and the Brigadier returned to Chester. Our
two companys, after getting a little refreshment at
Altringham, were joined by the other three from
Stockport. We were here informed that the advance
party of the highlanders had come into Manchester
last night and that their drums were heard this
morning, which was but six miles from us, so we
marched all five companys out about 12 o'clock, two
of them, viz, Stewart's and Campbell's were under
the command of Major Bendish to Lime (Lymm) that
night intending next morning to relieve the three at
Latchford with Colonel Gordon, and the other three
companys, viz, Spencer's, Mason's and Weakley's
went to High Lee (Leigh) to be at Frodsham, the
headquarters next day. When we came there the men
were pritty well quartered all about the country
houses, and the officers were received very civilly by
Mr. Lee (Leigh), a gentleman of fortune in that place
and were all invited to supper and lye that night at
his house, which gave us all great joy. I had at that
time got little or no sleep for the three nights past,
but alas, what a disagreeable message did we receive,
just as we were settling down to an elegant supper.
We received a letter from Major Bendish, inclosing
Colonel Gordon's orders for us all to come directly
to Warrington bridge to defend that pass, as he had
been informed that a party of the highlanders were
to be in town that night, so we gave orders for the
drum to bett 'to arms' and after eating a little with
the good gentleman, we marched all the men off with
great spirits, they all expecting to have a battle that
night."

"At about 12 o'clock we got to Latchford where we
found all the other five companys. That night, instead
of Mr. Lee's comfortable lodgings that we had made
ourselves so happy in expecting, we were forced to
put up on dale floor and sometimes a chair to sleep
in. The men provided themselves the best way they
could, in barns and stables."

(Manchester Central Lib.)

St. Annes Square, Manchester
The highlanders encamped here

"Next morning we found the information·we got was false and no highlanders appeared, on ye otherside however we heard by a man who came over from the town in the only boat that was then within some miles of us, and had been amongst them at Preston and Wiggan, and that they certainly intended to come to Warrington, and he believed the main body would be there against 12 0'clock this day. Upon that information we called a councill, having first made a strict inquiry into the man's character and found it to be very good from severall of the most creditable people in that place. We concluded that it was not safe for us to lye any longer there, as the frost had so lowered the river, that it was fordable in several places both above and below us, and as so small a body as ours lying there could be of no service in opposing the whole army, when there was no force near to support us in case we were bet from the post. About half an hour after we were informed from the other side that a considerable party of the enemy had been within 2 miles of us, but were since turned off towards Manchester.

In Manchester itself a different scene to that in Liverpool was being enacted; a town similar in size with about 20,000 people, but there the similarity ended. While Liverpool was staunch Whig and practically 100% Hanoverian, Manchester had more orthodox religious and political viewpoints.

The origins and backgrounds of the two peoples were also different, this contributing to their sympathetic leanings. Manchester folk were mainly of Saxon origin and agricultural stock, whereas Liverpool had a Celtic coastal influence, consequently creating different cultures and allegiances. The balance of religious views was also different.

There was a large Catholic population due to the country folk who had flooded into the new manufacturing town seeking work from the poverty of the farmsteads.

There were also, like Liverpool, many wealthy Catholic landowners residing around Manchester, but within the town there was a large influential High Church following. Ironically, there

(Manchester Central Lib.)

Market Street Lane, Manchester
Prince Charles made his quarters here at the home of Mr. Dickenson

was an allegiance between the two, caused by the Whig government's religious legislation which alienated Catholic and High Church alike. A change of King would benefit both Tories and Romans. They became fellow sympathisers for the Jacobite cause.

At this time Manchester was the hive of Lancashire disaffection. One, a Doctor Deacon, a nonjuring clergyman, who had a chapel or conventicle in Fennel Street, was the leader of the Jacobites. He was said to be in the confidence of the clergy of the collegiate church (now the cathedral), who were undoubtedly strongly suspected by their diocesan, Bishop Peploe, of treasonable practices, and, as subsequently appeared, not without cause. The agent of the Pretender was Colonel Francis Towneley (who had been recruited to the ranks at Preston) who, though a Roman Catholic, was in intimate association with the collegiate clergy. As a specimen of the party feeling of the period, it may be mentioned that a clergyman named Richard Assheton was about this time elected chaplain by the fellows, but rejected by the warden on the grounds, as admitted by himself, that he would never enter a tavern called "The George" and never baptize a child by that hated Hanoverian name.

Convivial meetings of the adherents of the Stuarts, which many of the clergy attended, were regularly held in different taverns in Manchester and its environs, at which the health of the king "over the water" was drunk in toast pottle deep. By now, many of the Hanoverian supporters had fled the town upon the approach of the rebels, but the Jacobite supporters congregated in great crowds offering them a hearty welcome.

The main body of the Scots army arrived on the 29th November and encamped in the recently constructed St. Anne's Square. Ahead of them, rode Prince Charles dressed in a light plaid, belted with a blue sash, who set up his own quarters at the home of Mr Dickenson in Market Street Lane.

A regiment was raised in Manchester as in Liverpool, but of course it was for the service of the opposite side. Lord George Murray quickly fixed his headquarters at the Dog Inn in Deansgate for the distribution of French commissions to officers. These were eagerly sought, that of a captain being sold for £50. Three sons of Dr. Deacon were officers in the corps. Thomas Syddall, son of the barber who took so conspicuous a part in the rising of 1715, was

adjutant, and made an active and able officer. One of the first
enrolled was Captain Jemmy Dawson, and Rev. Thomas Coppock,
of Brazenose College, Oxon, a teacher in the grammar school, was
appointed chaplain. Dressed in full canonicals, he accompanied a
drummer through the town, and exhorted the townsmen in the
name of God to enlist in the service of their rightful sovereign.
The regiment mustered about 500 strong, Colonel Towneley being
appointed their C.O.

On Saturday November 29th, the Prince was proclaimed in St.
Anne's Square amidst loud applause. The Rev. Mr. Clayton, one
of the chaplains of the collegiate church, offered prayers for the
new King in the public street of Salford. The rejoicings and
festivities of the day were closed with fireworks in the evening.
On Sunday, November 30th, a grand demonstration was held.

Being St. Andrew's Day, service was celebrated in the collegiate
church according to the liturgy of the Scottish Episcopal Church.
The new Manchester regiment mustered in the churchyard, their
flag inscribed "Church and Country". The men mounted blue
and white cockades, and the officers wore waistcoats of Stuart
tartan. Ladies with tartan ribbons, plaids and shawls, crowded
the church and paraded the streets. In the church, Prince Charles
occupied the warden's seat, and Mr. Coppock preached a sermon
from the text "The Lord is King, let the earth be glad thereof".
The demonstration created such enthusiasm that the Hanoverian
adherents were entirely cowed and, for the time being, withdrew
from the scene.

In the late afternoon of the 29th November, Lt. Shairpe wrote in
his diary ...

> "We arrived about 4 o'clock at Frodsham where we
> were greatly alarmed by a drum beating `the march'
> out of town, which was first heard by our Sgt. Major
> as he was going to fix a guard upon the bridge, who
> as soon as he heard it came in a great hurry to the
> house where the officers were quartered and informed
> us that he had heard the `march' beating over the hill,
> and believed the highlanders to be at hand, upon
> which we all got ourselves ready as soon as was
> possible, with our drums beating `to arms' and in 15
> minutes we marched 400 men down to the bridge,

Deansgate Manchester
Where Lord Murray had his headquarters for the recruitment of the Manchester Regt.

(Lv R.D.)

which was the most that we had in town, the rest being all quartered in the country, and there we found it to be a false alarm, raised by a boy who was learning to beat, and had gone there for that purpose. However this was of some service to us, as it gave us an opportunity of trying the mens' courage, which was very extraordinary as not a man of them showed the least sign of fear, but went all on with the greatest alacrity although I believe every one of them expected to be attacked that moment. The Lt. Colonel and Major were very well pleased with their behaviour. We fixed a guard that night of 100 men at the Bridge House.

The following morning the regiment received orders from Brigadier Douglas for one of the companies to stay at Latchford to defend the bridge and two other companies to march to Northwich.

The Liverpool regiment, aware that the Scots were about to cross the Mersey somewhere south of Manchester, was perplexed at these latest orders: the garrison command at Chester had persisted in dividing the regiment into individual companies, and now at the very time that preparations should be in hand for a possible confrontation with the enemy, orders to split the regiment came again. The "Blues" who were of the opinion they could march and meet the rebels at Northwich (if Chester be their destination), and should be a full strength regiment rather than a divided force, which would clearly be more advantageous in the event of a battle. Feelings now ran so high amongst the officers and men, that Lt. Shairpe wrote bitterly ...

"...when we heard (the orders) it appeared so odd a scheme to the whole core of officers, that we could not help complaining of it; and layed the blame of it all upon Lord Cholmondley, as we were told that he was very much averse to our coming into his garrison of Chester, for fear of the high pay our men had, raising some disturbance in his new regiment, and we had reason to believe he had been very instrumental in hindering us from joining the King's army and likeways that he had talked very freely of

our regiment in general, for which reasons we had
contracted a great dislike to him, as we looked upon
our regiment to be greatly superior to his. We
therefore resolved to show some little spirit and not
allow ourselves to be made fools of, or thrown into
danger when we could not be of any service and drew
up a remonstration to Brigadier Douglas which
Colonel Gordon took to Chester complaining of its
being very hard for us to be tossed all over the country
and not suffered to join any other force when the
enemy was so very near us, and more, that they would
not even allow us to keep together, but scattered us
all about the country in small parties which rendered
us quite defenceless against the most inconsiderable
attack. We concluded with telling him that we
thought if our service was not thought worth
accepting, we did not think it worth offering, only
desired he would let us know, that we might lay down
our arms in the same manner as we had taken them
up; as we did not choose to throw ourselves away
foolishly and be of no use at the same time by doing
it."

It appears that the Liverpool men were nearer to the truth than
they realised. Apparently, unknown to them, Col. Graham had in
his possession a letter he received, probably at Warrington, from
Lord Cholmondeley (sent on 15th November) suggesting some
reluctance to have the regiment at Chester, but certainly had no
hesitation in using them to defend the approaches to his garrison.
The letter stated ...

"Sir I received the favour of your Letter of the 14th,
in answer to which I must tell you, that it is no ways
in my Power, or Cognizance, the quartering of Troops,
without I receive the King's particular order for that
purpose; and indeed considering that my Regiment
is quartered here already and that 18 Regiments are
coming from the South, under the command of Sir
John Ligonier, the first of which may be expected in
five or six days at farthest, I cannot att all think it

adviseable for you to advance any further than
Warrington with the Regiment under your Command,
but to keep that Post and Quarter your Men in that
Town, and the Neighbouring Places.

"I communicated your Letter to the Mayor and Civil
Officers of this Corporation who besides the Objection
of your not having any quartering order signed by
the Secretary at War, alledge so many other reasons
for your not coming to this place, as I flatter myself,
must determine you to what is above advised.

"I shall be proud of hearing from you from time to
time, and shall allways take care to communicate
what orders I have from above that may be necessary
for you to know; I am With True Esteem Sir,

Cholmondeley"

His Lordship appears to have acted upon this letter of the 15th
November, but since then Brig. William Young had issued orders
for the Blues to withdraw to Chester*, (after the Mersey bridges
had been demolished.) With the enemy so close, the frustration of
the Liverpool Blues volunteering to fight for the King as a regiment
must be appreciated. Firstly, they had first been split into
companies to act in the role of a militia and then given a variety of
orders which appeared to come from various quarters many which
were contradictory. But the main bone of contention was failure
to recognise and give them the opportunity to act as a regiment.

At Manchester the Scottish army held its War Council and
deliberated on the next stage of the campaign.

The situation was not developing as many of them had envisaged.
The French had not invaded to assist them as originally planned,
nor had there been any sign of an English or Welsh uprising. There
had been no popular revolution to swell their numbers and it was
only Manchester that had displayed any loyalty to the young
Prince. Doubts had begun to creep in at Preston, and many in the
Highland camp voiced their concern with the obvious questions.
Where were the Stuart supporters from the mountains of Wales?

What had happened to the legions of English Jacobites from the
northern counties?

---

* See Cholmondeley letter of 24th November

No insurrection had materialised; in fact, there had been little support in general. The attitude of people south of the border had been one of apathy, the majority being neither fanatical Hanoverians nor Stuarts and there appeared very few eager to show military support for either side. It was a case of both sides "sitting it out" to see how the situation developed.

Cheshire was another county, again, with many Jacobite supporters. Would more rally to the Stuart standard as they advanced even further?

Perhaps the Highland forces had decided to march on London all along; or maybe they had left their options open, deciding upon events as they unfolded. But after Manchester it was confirmed: a direct march to London.

Lord George Murray, however, set about concentrating all efforts to maximise attention on the repair of the *Crossford* Bridge, the link between Manchester and Altringham and the road to Chester and the West; it was the beginning of his plan to out-manoeuvre the English forces.

The Scots pressed local workmen into felling poplar trees and commandeered horses and carts and took away ropes and chains; they took timbers and planking from a local timber yard and had the Stretford country people working throughout the day and night. In the darkness they worked by the light of torches and were given food and drink on site, in a non-stop haste to complete the crossing.

At 6 a.m. on Sunday 1st December, the first foot soldiers were making their way across, although only about 200 horse and foot soldiers eventually made their way towards Knutsford. They did so creating a lot of commotion.

General Bland, an English Officer writing from his headquarters at Newcastle-Under-Lyme to Lord Sempill at Stone and Lord Herbert at Shrewsbury, indicated that his out-scouts had observed the rebels making their way over the Crossford Bridge onto the Chester Road and west. "Pushing for Wales" he wrote, but considered they may go "by Shrewsbury or Wrexham but doubting they would attempt Chester".

This relatively small contingent of horse and foot soldiers emphasised and exaggerated every movement in an endeavour to draw maximum attention to themselves, whilst the main body of the Highland army, wagons and artillery, struggled across the

(Chester Arch Soc. & Chester R.O.)

Chester 1749
*Castle - Dee Mills and St. Johns Church -
Old Dee bridge (background).*

Mersey at Stockport and Cheadle Ford and marched direct south on the road for London.

At Frodsham, Lt. Shairpe wrote on 30th November and 1st December ...

"This night we received a letter from Colonel Graham at Northwich, ordering us to march the whole battalion to that place, there to wait the Duke's further command and the same (night) we had a letter from Colonel Gordon with an account of the success of our remonstration, which had had the intended effect, as we got leave from Lord Cholmondley to march us into Chester, however at that time we dispised that liberty as the order we had got from the Duke was much more agreeable. But in the night time we had a second letter from Colonel Graham countermanding ye first, as he thought it dangerous to lye at Northwich, having had certain intelligence of the highlanders crossing the Mersey by a wooden bridge, they had thrown over near Crossford. So in the morning (1st December) about 10 o'clock we marched for Chester, having been first joined by Captain Mason's Company which had gone to defend the pass at Warrington; and about three, we got into Chester along with the two companys that were ordered to Northwich, viz, Campbell's and Weakley's...."

Positioned at Northwich, Colonel Graham had suddenly needed to change his plans for the Blues. His intentions had been to march the regiment south and rendezvous with the Duke of Cumberland's army. But at 2.30 a.m., his out-scouts had reported that an advanced party of the rebels would be at Northwich within a few hours. Realising his Blues were on their way from Frodsham and could now meet head-on with the advanced companies of the Scottish army, he countermandered his original order and instructed that they now march into Chester where he would follow. The "Blues" grudgingly turned West and marched to the garrison town.

At least two newspapers at that time carried the news of the Scots march towards Wales and the West. The London Evening Post for 26th/28th November and the St. James Gazette for 3rd/5th December reported that "...they design for Wales, and there expect foreign aid.

"In Chester, rumours and counter rumours were on everybody's lips and those in charge of the castle and town, unsure exactly which way the Jacobites would march, set about the final stages of defence. They were aware that Carlisle Castle had been unable to stem the Scots invasion into England and a more efficient defence programme was implemented to defend the gateway into Wales.

Lt. Shairpe was impressed with the defence and reported ...

> "...when we came in there, which was on the (Sunday) 1st December, we found the city and castle was put in the best posture of defence that was possible, as it was believed by everybody that ye highlanders designe was to march through that place on their road to Wales, where they expected a great many would joyn them."

The London Evening Post endorsing the defensive work reported on 23rd/26th November "...The Watergate, Northgate and sally ports were bricked up, with only a wicket* left at Eastgate and the Bridge, a subaltern had charge of these wickets and a main guard was kept in Bridge Street at the end of Common Hall Lane". It was also reported that 2 engineers had been sent from London "to begin a train battery in order to command the Bridge and Welch shore".

Lt. Shairpe reports the activities regarding guard duty ...

> "The troops that lay there were Bligh's Regiment of Foot, Lord Cholmondley's and Lord Goor's (Gower's), two new regiments, with whom we did our turn of duty by keeping constant and strong guards in the city with them, which was all we did

* Wicket - a small door or gateway within a wall
* Roodee - raised parade ground area

72

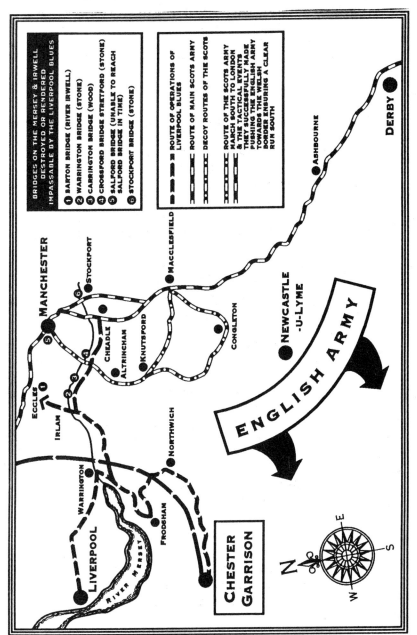

BRIDGES ON THE MERSEY & IRWELL DESTROYED OR RENDERED IMPASSABLE BY THE LIVERPOOL BLUES

1. BARTON BRIDGE (RIVER IRWELL)
2. WARRINGTON BRIDGE (STONE)
3. CARRINGTON BRIDGE (WOOD)
4. CROSSFORD BRIDGE STRETFORD (STONE)
5. SALFORD BRIDGE (UNABLE TO REACH SALFORD BRIDGE IN TIME)
6. STOCKPORT BRIDGE (STONE)

ROUTE OF OPERATIONS OF LIVERPOOL BLUES

ROUTE OF MAIN SCOTS ARMY

DECOY ROUTES OF THE SCOTS

ROUTE OF THE SCOTS ARMY MARCH SOUTH TO LONDON & THE TACTICAL EVENTS THEY SUCCESSFULLY MADE PUSHING THE ENGLISH ARMY TOWARDS THE WELSH BORDER ENSURING A CLEAR RUN SOUTH

MANCHESTER
STOCKPORT
MACCLESFIELD
CHEADLE
ALTRINCHAM
KNUTSFORD
CONGLETON
ECCLES
IRLAM
NORTHWICH
WARRINGTON
LIVERPOOL
FRODSHAM
NEWCASTLE-U-LYME
ASHBOURNE
DERBY

RIVER MERSEY

ENGLISH ARMY

CHESTER GARRISON

Murray's Manoeuvre outfoxed English army

73

extraordinary while we lay there, excepting one day
that the regiment was reviewed upon the Roodee* by
Lord Cholmondley who was very well pleased with
our performance during that time."

Amongst the many rumours flying around the garrison came
the bad news that on the 22nd November Lord John Drummond,
the Duke of Perth's brother, had landed in Scotland from France
with reinforcements to assist the Highland army.

As the Blues had marched into Chester, Lord George Murray
had marched rapidly west with his band of 200 men and met up
on the Chester Road with a group of English cavalry, who upon
seeing the Highlanders retreated south towards Newcastle-Under-
Lyme with confirmation of the rebels' progress "towards Wales".

Murray's diverting unit then did a sharp manoeuvre east and
down the Ashbourne Road via Leek to rendezvous with the main
body of the Scottish army marching towards the town of Derby.
The Duke of Cumberland and his English advisors based at
Stafford had been completely outfoxed. By the 3rd December most
of the Highland army were now at the town of Derby and in a
position to press on for London.

On Wednesday 4th December, Prince Charles called for a Council
of War with all his officers and advisors at his headquarters, Exeter
House. The time had come to decide exactly what action should
now take place - would it be prudent to advance on London or
should they return, back to Scotland?

Lord George Murray opened the debate by advocating a "return
to Scotland", arguing that his advisor, Colonel Ker of Graden, had
reported to him that the Duke of Cumberland with the English
army at Stafford (only 32 miles from them as the crow flies) had
an estimated force of 2,200 horse soldiers and 8,250 foot. Moreover,
the Duke, realising he had been outmanoeuvred would now be
closing in on them.

Marshall Wade in the North East had begun his march south and
east of the Pennines, but progress was slow due to weather
conditions; in London, a third army of volunteers was being formed
for the defence of the capital itself; in total a combined English
force of about 30,000 men. The same arguments were discussed
at Derby as at Manchester.

They despaired over the discouraging response of the English Jacobites and puzzled equally that there had been practically no opposition either, except for the destruction of the Mersey bridges by the Liverpool Blues. Their free access through the country, it was considered, was due to a lack of provocation by their orderly invasion.

Murray concluded by arguing that the English had not risen to support them, nor had the French assisted with a landing in the south as they had originally had indicated.

The Scots had done all that was required of them and they had come within a week's march of London; but to carry on without assistance now would be certain annihilation for both the Jacobite forces and the Prince. He proposed a return to Scotland and there to link up with Sir John Drummond's army and, if need be, make a stand on Scottish soil.

At least from Scotland there was positive news: the Highland army there was in control of the northern half of that country.

At the meeting all parties were at pains to convince the Prince of their utmost loyalty and support, but practically all members of the Council supported Murray's portrayal of the situation and assessment of the facts.

Prince Charles disagreed, with only one or two of his close aides supporting him. As usual he was fearless but foolish, advocating a march to Wales, despite no indication of support from that area.

A resolution was carried by a majority of the War Council that they would return North to join Sir John Drummond's forces. Prince Charles complained bitterly of betrayal, accusing Murray of turning the others against him.

The decision, to go further south though tempting, was impractical. To stand still or attempt to force their way west into Wales would mean an encirclement by the English forces and with no support, certain destruction - they turned back for Scotland.

The rank and file in particular felt their souls heavy and though appreciating it was the correct decision to return, the majority in their hearts considered it a disgrace "to turn their backs to the enemy". To them it was a point of honour; better to throw themselves at the English rather than the humiliation of turning about. It was lamented amongst the ranks "had we been beaten our grief could not have been greater".

Lord Murray attempted to lift their spirits and voluntarily took up the rearguard position - always considered the most dangerous position in a column - all the way back to Scotland, the Prince sulkingly ignoring him throughout the journey.

The climate had been dry and mild, for that time of year. As the Scots turned, so did the weather. The rains became incessant, the frosts heavier and biting winds came that struck chills into the bodies and hearts of the Highland men, whipping about them like an ice cold breath of some Celtic ill omen.

CHAPTER V

The rebel columns arriving back in Manchester on the 8th and 9th December were met with less enthusiasm on their return, and in some quarters outright hostility. Prince Charles, dismayed and angry at this change of attitude, slapped a fine of £5000 on the town (later reduced to £2000).

On the retreat, the forced marches left behind many stragglers wandering around the countryside. Some of these were of the Manchester Regiment who, already disillusioned by the rebels return to Scotland, had the added temptation of being close to home, to lure them from the ranks. Others completely alien to the area, alone or in small groups, got left behind. Those lost or exhausted were picked up by the country people and taken into custody. One such group after struggling across the Mersey met up with an armed group from Prescot.

A letter, written from that town relates the incident:

> "...Tuesday 10th December, a great number of our townsmen joined by above 100 farmers and other persons ventured armed with scythes, forks, guns and rusty swords to pick up what stragglers they could find of the rebel army and have since returned with above 40 of them, who are in a bad condition, being lame and almost dead with fatigue, they were yesterday, Friday 13th December, sent to different gaols for safety."

Some prisoners were confined in a barn later called the Scotts Barn in Scotchbarn Lane, where one prisoner is alleged to have hanged himself and been buried outside the barn.

Warrington also had a number of prisoners held in the town, imprisoned in the court house building temporarily, before being moved on again to various jails. They were described as "sitting barefooted on the floor, around a huge mess of oatmeal porridge which the whole party engaged in eating from the same dish". It is said "that they had with them a piper who kept up the spirits of the party by playing from time to time their favourite airs."

The Liverpool Blues spent from the 1st December to the 11th December at the Chester garrison in a tedious round of guard duties. While there, Lt. Shairpe recorded his view of the situation at Derby as seen from a soldier's point of view:

"The highlanders had marched as far as Darby, at Stone they had very nigh got past the Duke's army, but by his care and vigilance in marching by night to Swanson's Bridge pass* that they were necessitated to be masters of before they could go any further. He turned them there, and from that time forward they never offered to look southward again.

"Wednesday 11th December, we received orders from the Duke to march to Latchford to defend the old pass at Warrington bridge, and we got two small cannon for that purpose to prevent the enemy from returning that way while ye Duke followed them with his horse (cavalry). So about 12 o'clock that day we marched out of Chester as also did Brigadier Bligh's Regiment to joyn the army, and got to Frodsham about 5 o'clock where we haulted till eleven, when the Colonel gave orders for marching that night to Latchford, and so set out in a very dark cold night and got in about three in the morning (Thursday 12th December).

"I went to my old quarters at Mr Hall's which was extremely good for the place was warm and the men were almost starved with hunger and cold, having no quarters but what they could get in barns and stables. "Next morning the Regiment was drawn up, and three companys were ordered to stay at the bridge and the other five were sent into the country to be cantooned in the neighbouring villages and to be ready at a call. While we lay there, the Duke crossed the river about four miles above us with all his cavalry, in pursuit of the enemy who it was certain were now making the best of their way back again for Scotland. So as there was no further occasion for lying at Warrington Bridge, the Colonel sent Mr. McGough*

off to the Duke for further orders. He came back on
Saturday (14th December) night with orders for the
Colonel to march us to Preston and lye there till he
had occasion for us."

The newspaper, the Chester Courant, was reporting "...that various stragglers from the main Jacobite column were being taken
prisoner by the country people, and when they arrived in Chester
the wild appearance and the strange dress of the Scotsmen caused
amazement and curiousity."*

The Chester Courant also related that a soldier in the Liverpool
Blues apparently bored with the constant rotas of guard duty had
"gone absent" and found himself in the town of Wigan. Unfortunately he had got caught up with the retreating rebel army and
was now in great doubt of how to extricate himself from his difficulties. The paper reports:

> "...but being ready witted as well as nimble-fingered,
> he thought proper to take one of the rebels horses
> and furniture (harness etc.) together with a portman-
> teau (carriage) which was upon him, in which were
> clothes and other things to a considerable value and
> rode triumphantly with his booty back to his Regi-
> ment, which great piece of bravery excused his being
> punished as a deserter."

The Blues Regiment acquired a barge and Lt. Shairpe writes:

> "Sunday, being the 15th, we crossed the river by a
> "flatt" and about 11 o'clock marched out of
> Warrington for Wiggan, where we got in at 3 pm. But
> at 5 pm came 1000 volunteers of the Guards and other
> marching regiments back into town and Brigadier
> Bligh's Regiment, (which, with our men were all the
> infantry of the Duke's army). The cause of their re-
> turning, for they had only marched out in the morn-

─────────────────────────────

* A number of sources state that the Liverpool Blues actually took some stragglers prisoner
and into Chester but it wasn't the 2nd Company as Lt. Shairpe would certainly have mentioned it in his account.

ing and got half-way to Preston, it was a report the
Duke had heard, of 15 thousand French being landed
in the south, which may be reasonably said, was what
prevented our army from overtaking the highlanders, and threw them a day's march behind."

This report was instigated by organised rumours spread by English Jacobite sympathisers. It reached the Duke of Cumberland
that a French expeditionary force had put to sea from Dunkirk
and was threatening to land off the south coast of England. He
called a halt to his pursuing army, recalled General Oglethorpe
and returned the majority of his troops back to Wigan. This operation enabled the Prince to gain at least another day's march
ahead of the English forces.

The Duke, realising he had lost valuable ground made an attempt to overtake the rear guard of the highland army, by organising the sharp-shooters amongst the infantry to be mounted behind the cavalry men and these pressed on ahead of the main body
of the English force.

Whilst at Wigan Ensign Lee, who had conducted the recruiting
of the Blues in Liverpool, took over the adjutant's post, after Lieutenant Dunbar "threw it up" (presumably over some minor disagreement).

Shairpe complained about the lack of room in the town, due to
the mass of troops now billeted throughout all the houses and
anywhere that could accommodate them, they were glad when
morning came and they were able, with the rest of the army, to
march for Preston. He writes:

"We got all in there safe about three in the afternoon, where we found the first of the rebels that was
executed hanging in the market-place (whom the
Duke had seen tyed up that morning before he left
the town). The man had deserted from Sir John
Cope's army after the battle of Prestonpans and
joyned them.

"We haulted all the next day in Preston (13th December) as also did the rest of the Foot that came in
with us, and spent the night reviewing the men's arms
and ammunition and making more cartridges for
them. Next morning we all received orders to march
for Lancaster, and got there about four at night, where
Brigadier Bligh, who commanded the Foot, received
orders from the Duke to press horses and march them
all but our Regiment to Kendall with the utmost expedition*, which was accordingly done in the dark,
but (we) were then too late to be of any service, as it
was about the time that we got into Lancaster that
the scirmage was fought at Clifford,** which is upwards of 30 miles off."

This scirmage Shairpe relates to developed as follows:

The Highlanders had left Kendal, Prince Charles had declined to
ride any more, he dismounted and marched on foot ahead of his
clansmen, through the torrential rain and sleet. His example encouraged and spurred on the weary and dispirited Highlanders
in their long retreat. His men kept urging him to ride, declaring
they would follow just as readily, but the Prince declined and carried on walking with his troops. It was such actions as these that
enhanced his reputation (he was almost revered among the rank
and file), his comraderie and association alongside the ordinary
foot soldier developed eventually into a blind loyalty. Lord George
Murray was probably the only other leader of the Scots who could
command a similar loyalty, though with him it was recognition by
the soldiers of his military expertise, his powers of leadership and
a respect for him as an able commander.
These qualities were now being tested to the full. Since leaving
Derby he had commanded the rearguard of the column as he had
promised.

---

* It is possible the Duke left the Blues behind as a rearguard in the event of a French landing
or for accommodation purposes
** Clifton

It was a duty fraught with danger and for this reason it was considered highly honoured for each Regiment to guard this very vulnerable position, consequently each one had to take it in turn to protect the slow moving lumbering wagons and artillery at their rear.

True to his word he had stayed there, sometimes falling far behind the rapidly moving foot soldiers and most times a full day behind the main column. The usually atrocious roads of the north were made even more treacherous by the constant rain, the wagons constantly sinking to the axle boxes in the mud-filled ruts or lurching altogether from the narrow track roads into adjacent bog land.

Beyond Kendall and over the bleak moors towards Shap, the road rose ever higher, the dry stone walls on either side offering little shelter from the biting winds. The rain had turned to sleet soaking through the rough clothing of the ill-clad Highland men.

Plaids were wrapped about heads and shoulders and numb hands thrust deep into the folds of their encircling garments, where they clasped their muskets to their bodies in an attempt to keep the driving rain from the mechanisms.

The weather was dry and brighter on Wednesday 18th December. Lord Murray, upon hearing that the English cavalry were now only one mile to the rear of his column, decided it was time to resort to a delaying tactic, or the rearguard would be soon overrun.

He sent ahead for reinforcements and gathered 200 of John Roy Stewart's Edinburgh men, the Stewarts of Appin and the MacPhersons, in all 1,000 men to hold the English. Visibility had improved and he was able to take fresh stock of the situation.

Murray had requested more assistance from the Prince, but Charles was for pressing on to Carlisle and in fact instructed him to follow with all speed, but of course it was now too late for that. To retreat at this hour would mean the rear ranks of the column being overrun by Cumberland's cavalry.

Lord George Murray decided to make his stand 2 miles south of Penrith at the village of Clifton. Beyond the houses, north out of town the roadway was 20 feet wide and enclosed by dry stone walls either side. Beyond these the fields were squared off, again by walls and ditches, and finally the vast rugged moorlands, sprawling into the misty distance.

The Highland men took up positions in the narrow lane and on both sides, hiding in the darkened ditches and blending into the long shadows of thorn bushes and shrubbery as the late afternoon darkened.

This rearguard action would give the artillery and cumbersome ammunition wagons valuable time. Murray hoped to hold the English long enough for the Scots to get a clear day's march ahead. Cumberland's advanced troops, consisted of cavalry and foot soldiers. From the Regiments of Colonels Bland, Kerr, Cobhams, Montagu and Kingston.

There was no room for battle field formations and by the time both sides had decided their tactics and determined the strengths of the opposition the daylight had practically gone; the moon now shining brightly at times and then dipping behind dark clouds, creating moving shadows across the half-lit moorland.

Firing commenced about 5 pm, both sides shooting blindly and attempting to pick out their enemy by their gun powder flashes. After this initial spasmodic musketry fire a volley rang out from the English ranks, then silence, indicating the recharging of firearms.

It was during this brief respite that Lord Murray drew his sword and crying "Claymore" charged with screaming Highlanders at his heel and fell upon the English ranks with their usual murderous ferocity.

The Highlanders adopted a tactic of charge and retreat alternatively for a mile distance north of the village, the darkness finally closing in to the popping of musketry shots from both sides. Then finally the Scots slipped away into the blackness of the night, leaving the cries and moans of the wounded echoing about the still moor.

In the morning it was discovered that 10 English soldiers had died, another lingering and dying later[*] and 29 men were wounded.

The Scots had 5 killed. These were buried at Clifton at a place called the "Rebel Tree". 40 prisoners, some wounded, were taken the next day.

Both sides claimed a victory. The English considered they had

---

[*] Clifton Parish Registers

driven the Scots from their defensive position; the Scots arguing they had held the English and given their forward army precious time in their retreat.

It was the last battle on English soil, with both sides stating exaggerated figures of their opposite number killed and wounded.

The following day, the 19th December, the English forces pressed on north, leaving behind their comrades who had suffered horrific wounds by broadswords and taking prisoner the rebels who, in their turn, had been left behind by the retreating Scots, many with smashed limbs from musket balls.

At the time of this scirmage at Clifton, Lt. Shairpe was complaining to his diary about the "Blues" lack of action and on the 18th December he wrote:

> "This night and the two following days we lay in Lancaster and did nothing extraordinary but mount a Captain's guard at the end of the bridge, and a subaltern's in town, till on Saturday the 21st December, we received an order from the Duke about noon to march for Penrith directly, and there wait his further orders. This order came at a very unreasonable time, as we had all the men under arms a little before but (they) were then dismissed, which made it very difficult to get them all out again (being retired to their quarters); however the Colonel hurried away with a part of them, the rest followed after. They all reached Burton that night.
>
> "Next day we marched very early for Shapp and gott there late after a most fatigueing march, which was occasioned by our haulting in Kendall as we went through and the badness of the roads, as they are the worst that are, in that part of England. We were very badly quartered that night and set out next day to Penrith where we got ourselves pritty well refreshed, but got orders to march early in the morning to Stanwick Bank, a small village the other side of Carlisle and this end of the bridge there to defend the pass and prevent any of the enemy from making their escape that way, as we had information of 600 them

being left there while the Duke was to beseage the
town which he had now invested; and accordingly
we set out from Penrith in the morning where I left
my horse as we were informed the place we were
going to was fit neither for men nor beast to live in,
so I marched on foot all that day, which rained continually in a very bad country. When we came within
three miles of Carlisle we turned off to the right hand
in order to cross the river by Warwick bridge which
took us about five miles round and that night as it
continued raining very hard and began to grow dark,
we halted at a little village called Crosbie within two
miles of Stanwicks where we lay that night."

The Liverpool Blues had marched around Carlisle and were now
about to take up positions to the north of the town on the road out
to Scotland. By now of course Prince Charles and the vast majority of his army had crossed the border but he had left behind a
contingent to defend the garrison town and castle of Carlisle.

Charles had arrived at the city on the 19th December complete
with his heavy baggage, wagons and artillery with Lord George
Murray and those who had been involved at Clifton following 7
miles to the rear.

The bitterness between the Prince and Murray which had pre-
vailed from Derby continued at Carlisle with Murray withdraw-
ing for much of the time and keeping to himself. The rift continued with the Prince letting it be known that he considered that
Lord Murray had instigated the other officers into a decision to
return to Scotland.

Charles had decided to leave a garrison to hold Carlisle, again a
decision against the wishes of the majority of his advisers. Lord
Murray had advocated at the war council a proposal to blow up
the castle, carrying away all the stores possible, and everything
else to be dumped in the river. This was voted against and the
Prince's scheme was finally adopted by the Chiefs. Murray immediately volunteered himself, with the Atholl Brigade, to under-
take the task of holding the castle against the English forces.

He certainly had no recourse to prove his loyalty to the Prince
and he certainly had not altered his opinion on this course of action. It was obvious he wished to emphasise the futility of the

Carlisle S.W. view of Duke of Cumberlands battery positioned on the Primrose Bank

(Carlisle Tract Series).

Prince's proposal of holding Carlisle. For all the discord between the two the offer was refused. There was no way Prince Charles could afford to sacrifice his only general; he must have appreciated then that he would eventually lose Carlisle sooner rather than later, but there was no point in losing his best Field Commander and adviser as well, even though they were constantly at loggerheads with each other.

Col. John Hamilton was appointed to command the castle and Col. Francis Towneley volunteered to guard the city, a contingent of 270 Highlanders and Lowlanders with some French and Irish officers, a few Privates of Lally's Regiment and the remnants of his only English unit, 150 men of the Manchester Regiment. Towneley's offer to remain in the garrison must have reassured others who may have looked on the duty with apprehension.

It is difficult to reason with the Prince's decision to leave a garrison at all at Carlisle. In the short term he would be unable to return with reinforcements to relieve those at the castle, none being immediately available; and in the long term, being in flight into the Scottish heartland to regroup and recruit new forces would involve too much time. There were not enough supplies at the Garrison for a prolonged siege. Even Charles' advisers had estimated just a few days before Cumberland over-ran Carlisle. His aides had also discussed the heavy rains, incessant at that time, pointing out that the rivers in the area would soon be unfordable, creating a natural barrier against the pursuing English troops, but it also meant any Scots army would encounter the same difficulties should they attempt to relieve the garrison. Also if those inside the city, should they attempt to break out from the siege, they too would meet the same problem of the rivers in full flood.

It would seem he was pleased to sacrifice the garrison of 400 men to enable him a clear run into Scotland. When a series of rearguard style actions which had been successful at Clifton could possibly have had the same delaying effect, without the loss of so many personnel.

Consequently on the 20th December the Scots army had, on the Prince's 25th birthday, crossed the River Esk and into Scotland, abandoning his loyal followers at Carlisle. His attitude as usual was cavalier, but credit must be given to his leadership and for his ability and motivation in getting the majority of his army back home intact.

This certainly had been an accomplishment. In less than a fort-night the whole of the Scottish Army which consisted mainly of foot soldiers had withdrawn intact over a distance of 200 miles. They had been hotly pursued by cavalry and by a considerable army which could not quite intercept them due to their rapid and well disciplined retreat. The weather conditions were appalling in the extreme. If it was not snowing it was raining in torrents. The men suffered cold and fatigue and, above all, disappointment and disillusionment. Despite the tribulations they had endured, their retreat had been a military success.

The castle at Carlisle was an old irregular building nearly 700 yards in circuit. Its armaments were 20 pieces of iron cannon six pounders and also some smaller guns. The walls were not par-ticularly solid, in fact several had large cracks in them. There was no moat or ditch except on the town side which was nearly filled up. There was no outworks or flanks. The drawbridge at the main south entrance was too accessible and the only single gate extremely vulnerable. Adding to this precarious situation was the lack of foodstuff, the retreating army taking the majority of it with them.

Inside the castle the Scots and the Manchester men were taking stock of the situation. First they attempted to put the walls into some kind of serviceable condition by making sandbags and earthenworks constructed to supply the defective rampart; spikes were impaled at the gate and the cannons were manoeuvered into the best defensive positions. But for all their efforts it was obvi-ous that the defence could not withstand a heavy artillery bom-bardment. Cumberland, after viewing the castle called it an "old hen coop", which he would bring down about their ears and com-menced preparations to do just that.

He immediately despatched orders to the port of Whitehaven to procure cannon from the shipping merchants and surveyed the high ground outside Carlisle for the purpose of raising artillery batteries against it..

On the rise of land to the west of the castle, called the Primrose Bank, the Duke with his advisers marked out the site for 2 batter-ies of cannon with a trench leading to each position. Whilst en-gaged in these operations the Duke was fired on from the castle and only narrowly escaped the shot which passed between him-self and the engineer in charge.

The "Blues" spent Christmas Eve sleeping in their wet clothes, some of them amongst livestock in stables and chicken coops; the officers huddled about the firesides of the small cottages of Crosbie village. It was a particularly uncomfortable night.

On Christmas Day, Wednesday 25th December, Lt. Shairpe wrote:

"We had orders to be at Stanwick before daylight as there was a rising ground we had to go over that was exposed to the fire from the castle, which they kept pritty constant to the side that the Duke lay on; but it was represented to us to be of greater danger to get to that place than it actually was, which made us take more caution in marching than there was need for. We got to Stanwicks Bank about 8 o'clock of Christmas morning, a wreched poor place to spend that time in, and found General St. George's Dragoons lying there, Bligh's Foot had marched from there that morning to go and joyn the Duke's army, which was cantooned on the west side of the town, as we came up to supply their place. As soon as the men were all come up, General Bland, who commanded on the Stanwick side of the river, gave orders for the four youngest companys to be quartered in two villages about half a mile distance and the other four companys to continue there, and were to be relieved in their turn. This day Captain Stewart's Company mounted the guard, being first upon command, and at night Captain Tongue's mounted a reserve guard (nothing extraordinary happened). That night orders were given by the General, for neither officer or soldier to go to bed, but always to be in readiness to turn out at a moments warning, which orders were continued all the time we lay in that place and were strictly observed by our regiment, as they had no place to lye in but the guard-rooms, the other houses being all took up by the Dragoons before we came."

The Liverpool men had joined St. George's Dragoons and a 1000 Dutch troops that had come overland from General Wade's army in the east. Work was completed on an earth work and trench defence at the foot of Stanwick Hill adjacent to the Priestbeck Bridge, defending the road out of the city to Scotland. As Lt. Shairpe reported "the work was carried out under incessant fire from the castle but the Blues were successful since the rebel gunnery was not, from all accounts, too effective. Although busy throughout the day, the 2nd and 3rd companies took over guard duty while the officers of the other 2 companies were to go the rounds ensuring all the men were alert and awake throughout the night.

> "The afternoon of the 26th December and the Duke came around to our side of the river to reconnoyter and went down by himself to view the castle and city, which was the first time I had seen him."

At this point no cannon had yet arrived for the English positions.
The same day the besieged garrison managed to push out a party of 80 men with a cannon and advanced through the Scotch Gate (facing the Stanwick Bank) and onto the Eden Bridge, and under-cover of fire were able to drive into the city a flock of sheep, which had been grazing in the lowland between the walls and Stanwick Bank to supplement the dwindling rations inside.

Appreciating the desperation of those inside, Cumberland cut the mill races and rivers stopping the water supplies to the mills which lay outside, but close against, the westwall (on his side of the city). These had been effectively providing flour to the Jacobite forces inside the walls.

That night some of the English troops took lodgings in a house outside the wall at the south end of the town, near the English gate and Colonel Towneley appreciating it may prove dangerous if permitted to be established, blasted it with the citadel guns reducing it to ashes.

> "Our companys were relieved in the morning by Captain Tongue's and Stewart's and we were ordered to do the same duty as they were on the day before; about 12 o'clock that night we were aroused and were all out under arms, the main and reserve guard marched down to the trenches, the alarm being raised

by a sentry upon this end of the bridge, where there was a guard continually kept (of a troop of Dragoons and a detachment from our reserve guard of an officer and 25 men) who, having seen several people come over the walls and they had quite left off passing the word round the garrison. This silence made us suspect that they intended making a sally that night. We stood under arms about an hour and fired a few shots off to let them know we were in readiness to receive them, but they all kept quiet so we ordered the men in again and sent a party to a ford below, to see if there were any of them making their escape that way, but they met with none."

wrote Lt. Shairpe

On Friday the 27th December by the exertions of the country people of the surrounding districts six 18-pounders were now brought up from Whitehaven and placed in position on the Primrose Bank.

Lt. Shairpe continues:

"At that time also came in a waggon with four coehorns from General Wade's army, and a little after, we began playing them from the trenches. This night we threw about 25 shells, which mostly fell either in the town or castle and brought a very hot fire upon the place, yet the trench-guard was kept in. While I was going the visiting-round there, they fired a round of grape or case-shot, which fell very thick about us, but nobody was hurt as we were pritty well sheltered by the trenches.

"Upon Saturday morning, 28th December, about 8 o'clock, the Duke opened his battery, which was situated upon the rising ground on the west side of the castle and consisted of six 18 pd cannon which he had from Whitehaven. Their fire was returned very briskly from the castle from a 4 gun battery, which they continued all this day very warmly, and now and then they let a shot fly to our side when our men appeared over curious in looking at them, which they

*"Liverpool Blues" north view of
Carlisle from Stanwick Bank.
Priestbeck bridge and Eden bridges in foreground.*

(Carlisle tract series)

were very frequently, being now growing quite bold
by nobody being hurt."

Cumberland divided his firepower into 2 groups of 3 guns, pre-
directed against the 4 gun battery of the castle at its north end and
the other 3 against the battery situated on the west wall directly
behind the castle mills.

The rampart of the castle's 4 gun battery was very low and afforded no protection to the gunners although an earthwork barrier had been raised to offer them cover. The Duke's cannon speed-
ily demolished this and by now not a man could stand there. The
Duke's fire continued unabated throughout the whole day.

The north side of the castle was also under fire from the English
positions on Stanwick Bank, but the dangers at Stanwick was not
only cannon fire from the castle; but because of the angled north
wall of the fortress, cannon shot could be deflected from
Cumberland's "Primrose" battery in the west, ricocheting into the
English ranks at Stanwick. Some cannon shot in fact careering
through the arches of the Priestbeck Bridge with Lt. Shairpe relating:

> "Our Colonel had a very narrow escape as he was
> going past the guard that I was upon, a shot being
> fired from the 6 gun battery, the ball just missed him
> and broak a tree that was hard by. This night all our
> four companys were upon guard and the coehorns
> were thrown as formerly."

Also throughout the night the rebels were also active and managed to make good the earthenwork in front of their 4 gun battery
on the north wall. Come daylight of Sunday morning of the 29th
December they were able to commence firing from that position
once again, both sides bombarding each other continually.

Into the morning the Duke's batteries slackened as they were
running out of cannon ball, but by 2 pm a fresh supply had arrived and the firing again became vigorous once more. That
evening one of the walls was observed to totter and it was about
this time the rate of firepower lessened from the castle.

·"This night 4 more 18 pdrs came up from
Whitehaven to the Duke, and when dark they began
making a battery of them, some little nearer the castle than the other which was completed next morning. I was all this night upon the trench-guard, and
as I marched my detachment down, the castle fired
guns at our coehorns which were just then throwen,
but did no damage. We kept close to the fence and
heard the ball fly over us. These were the last shots
that the enemy fired, being very quiet all night."

When the garrison, upon seeing at first light on the 30th December this new battery of cannon that had been so hastily constructed
overnight, they realised that their fate was sealed. A messenger
was sent out with two letters, one from Governor Hamilton to the
Duke offering surrender of the place on condition of the garrison
being allowed the privileges of prisoners of war, the other addressed to the Commander of the Dutch troops by the French officer in the town, summoning the Dutch Commander to retire with
his troops from the English army. In accordance with the terms of
the "Capitulation of Tournay" no attention was paid to either letter and the messenger was taken into custody.

Later that day they hung out the white flag and called out over
the walls that they had hostages, ready to be delivered at the English gate.

Upon this the Duke sent Colonel Conway and Lord Bury with
the following messages:

i) His Royal Highness will make no exchange of
    hostages with rebels and desires that they will
    let him know what they mean by hanging out
    the white flag.

ii) To let the French Officer know, if there is one in
    the town, that there are no Dutch troops here,
    but enough of the Kings to chastise the rebels
    and those who dare to give them assistance.

Signed: Colonel Conway
Aide-de-Camp to H.R.H. The Duke

Item (ii) of the message was of course a blatant lie as 1000 Dutch troops were quartered with the Liverpool Blues Regiment over on Stanwick Bank. Even so it was a fact that there were enough English to take the garrison. Two hours later the following answer was returned:

"In answer to the short note sent by His Royal Highness Prince William Duke of Cumberland, the Governor, in name of himself and all the officers and soldiers, gunners and others belonging to the garrison, desire to know what terms His Royal Highness will be pleased to give them, upon surrender of the city and castle of Carlisle, and which known His Royal Highness shall be duly aquainted with the Governor and garrisons last or ultimate resolution; the white flag being hung out on purpose to obtain a cessation of arms for concluding such a capitulation. This is to be given to His Royal Highness' Aide-de-Camp.

Signed: John Hamilton

Immediately Colonel Conway and Lord Bury were sent back with the following terms:

"All the terms His Royal Highness will or can grant to the rebel garrison of Carlisle are that they shall not be put to the sword, but be reserved for the King's pleasure.

"If they consent to these conditions the Governor and principal officers are to deliver themselves up immediately and the castle, citadel and all the gates of the town are to be taken possession of forthwith by the King's troops. All the small arms are to be lodged in the town guard-rooms and the rest of the garrison are to retire to the cathedral, where a guard is to be placed over them. No damage is to be done to the artillery, arms or ammunition. Headquarters at Blackhall, December 30th, half past two in the afternoon by His Royal Highness' Command.

Signed: Richmond, Lenox and Aubigny
Lt. General of His Majesty's Forces

95

The siege was over, but within the walls another conflict was raging, this time between the 2 Commanders, Colonel Towneley of the Manchester Regiment and the Governor Colonel Hamilton. Towneley vehemently rounding on him for surrendering and not making a defence to the last, he declared "that it was better to die by the sword than fall into the hands of those damned Hanoverians". His words helped to bring about his end at his subsequent trial.

At Stanwick The Liverpool Blues, now suffering the fatigue of continual duties, were too tired to celebrate the news that the siege was finally over, but the realisation there was no loss to their numbers brought a satisfactory and silent relief amongst those huddled in the mud-filled trenches. Shairpes account says:

"This day (Monday 30th December) was spent in sending off messages to and fro till it was night, when all the Foot with the Duke marched into the city at the Irish gate, and at the same time Stewart's 4th Company of our own regiment, and 60 Dragoons of St. George's dismounted and went and took possession of the Scotch gate. The city had surrendered to the Duke upon no other terms than leaving themselves at the King's mercy. So that night a message was sent to London to know his pleasure.

"Our three companys that were still at Stanwick mounted guard that night in three different places, and the trenches were filled up to have an easier communications with the town. Next day nothing extraordinary happened, only the Duke entering the town, at which time all the guns in the castle were fired.

"Orders were given by General Bland, that none of the officers nor soldiers on our side should offer to cross the bridge upon any reason whatever, which the men thought very hard, as they were very desirous to get into good quarters and curious to see the highlanders. Our 4 oldest companys had now been upon duty for six nights running without ever getting any rest or being relieved by the younger companies as it was first proposed, of which they made great complaints and indeed I must say, they had reason for it, as they were now growing sick in great numbers, and quite stupid for want of rest. However there was no redress for them.

"This day (31st December) at noon our company was ordered to mount the Main guard, which went very ill down with us; however we resolved to make no complaint, as we looked upon this to be the last scene of our hardship. Had not the town surrendered, when indeed it did this would have been a turn of much harder duty than it was, being a very easy one, having nothing now to fear, as this was the time the Duke had fixed upon to storm the breech of the castle, which would have been by this time pritty wide. His designe was, as I afterwards heard, to have attacked it with 800 Foot, by detachment from all that were with him, so that our proportion of it would have been 100, but thank God that it happened as it did, else a good many lives would have been lost in the attempt."

Highland Soldier
Shown wearing belted-plaid and multi tartans.

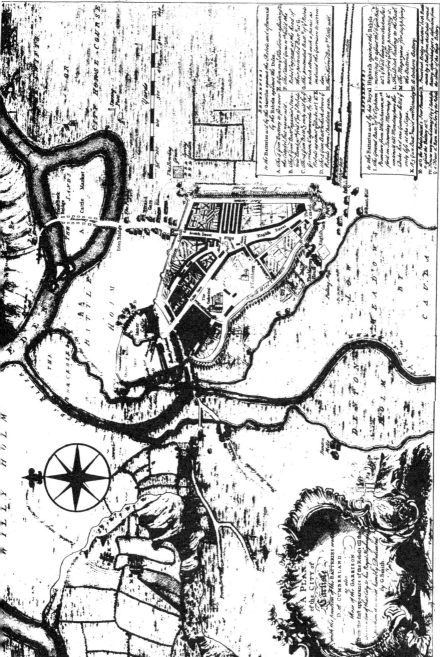

Carlisle showing English battery positions

(Cumbria R.O.)

Volunteer Soldier "Liverpool Blues"

CHAPTER VI

Lt. Sharpe's Diary continues....

"Next morning, the 1st January we were all ordered to be under arms by eight in the morning and marched off from Stanwick by nine. As we marched in review through the town past the Duke, the officers all saluted him with their half-pikes as they went past him, and Colonel Graham stood by and gave him a character of us, which I believe was fully as good as we deserved. He gave the Colonel orders to march us directly for Liverpool and there wait for further orders.

"So that night we reached Penrith, but an accident happened to me, which I was afterwards very glad of, as by it I had an opportunity of returning to Carlisle and there saw all the prisoners, castle and such that was worth seeing. Captain Spencer had sent his servant, the day after the town surrendered to Penrith for his own and my baggage, which we had left there, not to be troubled with it at the seage. But the people whose care it was in had sent it some days before to the Duke's quarters, thinking it belonged to the forces with him; which the servant came up and informed us of upon the march about 2 miles out of town. So I returned back again and found the baggage and followed them to Penrith after I had diverted myself some time amongst the prisoners, but had a troublesome journey of it, as the old horse I borrowed (my own being left at Penrith) grew tired about halfway to Penrith and obliged me to walk on foot the other half in the dark."

"Next morning we marched from Penrith. The Duke of Cumberland overtaking us at about 11 o'clock, carrying on at a fast pace for London. (There being another report of a French landing in the South.) We got into Kendall pritty soon considering the distance to be 20 long miles. From there we marched to Lancaster in a day and next to Preston, where the Colonel thought proper to hault all Sunday, as the last four days had been very hard upon the men, but the weather was then too good to leave a day of it, at this time of year, and we having had nothing but fine and dry from when we left Carlisle.

"At Preston we found Lord Halifax's and the Marquis of Granby's Regiments, two new ones, but very good looking men, which with the quarters taken for the 4 Troops of Ligonier's Horse that had marched with us from Carlisle had so filled the town that our four oldest companys were obliged to be quartered in the little villages near to town where there was good entertainment.

"Monday 6th January, we made a short march to Ormskirk, and as Tuesday was the post day at Liverpool, the Colonel went forward there and ordered the regiment to hault till we heard from him, as he was in great expectation of having the Duke's orders to continue the regiment, and if so he did not care to let them come into the town, but as nothing came that day he sent orders for us to march into town next morning. So on Wednesday the 8th, we returned to Liverpool, which unluckily hapened to be a very rainy day and disappointed us greatly in the appeal we intended to have made which would have been to the best advantage, as the men got their arms and cloathes very clean, but were now quite rusty and dirtied by the rain. We here mounted a Captain's guard and had the men out under arms every other day in the same manner as when from home, which was done weekly to keep the men together and in readiness if any orders should come from the Duke about establishing the regiment which the Colonel wished for very earnestly, as he was much greeved to think of disbanding so good a body of men at this time; however after having waited for some orders from the Duke as he had told the Colonel he would let him hear from him at Carlisle, and no answer coming to a letter the Mayor had wrote about taking the regiment into the King's pay as subscription mony was now almost spent, and consequently, we must either be disbanded or established immediately.

"The gentlemen of the town came to a resolution, but not with the consent of the Colonel, who would fain have persuaded them to continue the regiment some little time longer and that if they heard nothing by Tuesday's post they must be disbanded, as they say they must have an answer to their letter if the King had any thoughts of taking them into his pay, and that it was needless and very great expence to keep the men lying here idle and of no service.

"So on Tuesday the 14th January, no letter coming, we were ordered to be all out under arms in the Town field and there, the regiment being formed into a circle, the Colonel went about, along with the Mayor and such, made a short speech to every company, leting them know that they were now disbanded and at their own liberty to go where they pleased, but desired that they would stay in town in case the regiment should be raised again and that they should not enlist themselves in any other regiment for some time. After that, each company marched down to their Captain's quarters and there delivered up their arms and ammunition, received what pay was due to them and so were dismissed.

(Colonel Graham himself graciously refused payment of any kind from the Corporation.)

"The three Field officers stayed for some days in town to see what a little time would produce, but no orders coming they all returned to their respective posts, as also did the rest of the officers to their different employment in life.

"So here ended the history of the Liverpool Regiment during the time that I was engaged in this affair. I can't say that I ever before spent any time more agreeable and I am sure that most of the gentlemen that were with us will say the same with me. For

103

though we frequently had a great dele of fatique and
trouble in our marches and otherways, yet that was
always made more than amends for by the mirth and
joy that we afterwards had when we got into our quarters, and the constant harmony that we lived in with
one another, and I dare say most of the officers would
have had a great dele of pleasure in continuing longer
in that way of life if they had had the opportunity of
doing it in the same rank they were in; but there was
one thing which we all could not help looking upon
as ungratefull and not good usage, and that was the
government taking so little notice of us as not to answer the Mayor's letter, even after the Duke, as we
were certainly informed, had given a very great character of us in London, and as we were the best new
regiment raised in the kingdom upon the same occasion, and the very only one that had been of service
till then; yet was there 13 of the new ones established,
and we left out."

And so the short reign of the Liverpool Blues came to an end on
the 14th January*. Lieut. Shairpe was not quite correct regarding
the non-disbandment of the other volunteer regiments, some of
these units in fact lasted only a little longer, some for a few years.
Perhaps the end was in sight for the "Blues" when they made it
known that the subscription money was running low and a request was forwarded for them to be established as a regiment of
the line and consequently to be paid by the King.

Disbanded, the Liverpool men were treated as heroes and toasted
accordingly in the beershops and inns throughout the town. They
carried the name "Blue Boy" with pride for the rest of their lives.
Their stories being told and retold for generations about the firesides of the old town.

No other information appears forthcoming regarding Lt. Walter
Shairpe. Perhaps he joined another regiment to fight the foe, but
the curtains of time appear drawn behind him as he leaves the
stage of history.

* Although disbanded the exploits of the regiment lived on. Indeed, another Liverpool Blues regiment was formed in the year 1777 in honour of the original "Blues".
Again they were volunteers, but this time were accepted as Kings men and consequently these "Blues" wore red coats becoming the 79th Regiment of Foot and saw
service in the Carribean.

The other soldiers went back to their various trades and occupations about the town, some officers returning to their positions with the Corporation and administering the business of the town, others who were merchants resuming a direct conflict once again with France, fitting out privateers to hunt the enemy and to engage in daring battles at sea to win the lucrative prizes of war.

The three field officers returned to their old regiments, Colonel Graham being transferred on the 7th February from the (54th) 43rd Regiment to the 11th Regiment, which was then on service in the Scottish border country. Within a few weeks he was promoted to Brigadier General. Lt. Col. Gordon returned to his old regiment commanding a regiment of invalids (veterans) until 1751. Major Bendish returned to the Marines, becoming a Lt. Col. in 1755, a Colonel in 1762 and retired as a Major General.

And what of Prince Charles and his Highland army? After crossing the border at Carlisle he rode on north with his proud mountain soldiers, his flamboyant personality winning supporters as his army marched into the heartland of Scotland.

The country was roughly divided across the centre into Highlands and Lowlands. Those in the Lowlands were comparatively "Anglicised" but the Highlanders were a celtic people speaking a foreign tongue, dressing and acting in a completely alien manner to their fellow Scots south of the Highland line.

These men from the glens looked on the Lowlanders in the same vein as they would the Englishmen and the men from the south in their turn considered the Highland man as a barbarian, a feuding cattle thief, unreligious and a threat to the progress of modern 18th century Scotland.

Prince Charles won few friends in the southlands but the further north he went more allies rallied around. Finally he had control of most of the north of Scotland and a loose support of some of the southern counties.

On Wednesday 16th April 1746 he took his troops up onto the ill-fated Drummossie Moor overlooking the town of Inverness, near Culloden House. There the proud and foolish young man faced the Duke of Cumberland's well disciplined cavalry and artillery and in Britain's last feudal battle he orchestrated the suicidal self-destruction of not only the Scottish army, but the eventual elimination of the clansman's way of life.

The defeat at Culloden was the end of Scotland's part in the

European war and also the battle that marked the beginning of the end of the tribal Highlanders. The English government were then able to systematically set about the neutralisation of the clan system.

From the mud and blood of this final battlefield and its bloody aftermath, the hopes and spirits of the people were only kept alive by a flickering glow of myths and legends, so that now we are left with only a romantic illusion rather than a reflection of a vanished way of life.

Liverpool also played its part in assisting the central government. We may criticise today the 18th century Liverpool man's motives (as indeed, all English people at that time), but Scotland and Ireland, because of its links through its religion with continental Europe, was always considered a constant threat to the stablility of England.

A fortnight after the Battle of Culloden Moor, Liverpool, like the other towns throughout England, was still celebrating victory over the Jacobites.

Church bells rang and their preachers offered up prayers on behalf of their congregations, thanking their Maker for the victory over the enemy and grateful that the French had not landed to enslave them. They expressed gratitude also for saving them from the Highland heathens, who had come so close to the town and, perhaps, have murdered them in their beds.

But the sermons of thanksgiving quickly became more vociferous with the relief of their survival, some sermons becoming sheer "incendiary".

The preachers fiery words and the tavern orators urgings soon had those from around the dockside areas thirsting for revenge. They staggered out into the narrow alleyways seeking vengence on the "Allies of Rome" living within their midst.

The frightened Catholic population immediately evacuated the area. They were taking no chances, although, throughout the emergency, they had not shown any support for the Pretender, even when it seemed imminent that he may invade the town.

But those living about the docksides now demanded retribution especially those with a quick eye for loot.The Mayor James Broomfield further provoked the situation when he became involved in a disagreement with a local priest, by antagonising the already heated situation even more.

The mob rose on the 30th April. Sailors, ships carpenters and the like stormed along Castle Street past the Exchange, along Old Hall Street and up Edmund Street to the Catholic Chapel that had been established there in 1727.

The rioters milled about the building and began to break their way in when suddenly a silence fell upon the mob as two priests, Father Mermenigild Carpenter and Thomas Stanley, confronted them. The mob behaved with the greatest respect to the two men and without noise or violence opened a passage through the crowd for Father Carpenter to go in to the altar and take various articles out of the chapel. The priests left the scene and after this the mob tore up the benches and made a bonfire of everything combustible in both the chapel and the priests' house and pulled down the whole of both house and chapel.

The town simmered and celebrated through early May, the majority still toasting the victory in Scotland. A minority still bent on retribution and an excuse for plunder rose again on the 20th. The mob this time reacted upon finding out that a Mrs Green* had used a room in her house as a chapel for the Blessed Sacrament. This house was attacked with even more venom that the Edmund Street Chapel, especially it was discovered that Mrs Green was the widow of a Captain Francis Green, who had joined Prince Charles. The fury of the crowd brought out the Mayor, the Town Clerk and a number of Police Officers.

These officials were driven away by the ferocity of the mob. The house was looted, all the valuables and furniture being carried away and the house set on fire.

Some of the gentlemen in the area managed to raise a force large enough, not only to extinguish the flames, but to prevent the destruction of other houses in the area. They were able to drive away the rioting "bandits" as the newspapers of the day called them.

Unfortunately, these incidents forced many of the peaceful catholics living in the area to sell of all their effects and leave the town.

These riots were not confined to Liverpool. They were happening in other towns, one example was Ormskirk where the chapel

---

* The unfortunate Mrs Green moved into a new house in Dale Street on 24th September and a little later a new chapel was established in Lumber Street disguised as a warehouse, the cost being implemented by Squire Nicholas Blundell of Little Crosby.

and mission house* was attacked and partially burnt down by the mob.

Here again the objects of the rioters anger did not appear to be the catholics themselves but more the chapels and symbols of what the rioting mob considered they represented.

With the Battle of Culloden over and the aftermath of the "cleaning up", all the prisoners were brought to England to be tried. The trials took place in the cities of London, York and Carlisle. Amongst these prisoners were the Manchester men, captured at the siege of Carlisle. They were the first to be brought to justice, their hearings taking place in the capital itself.

On 15th July Colonel Francis Townley, the 38 year Colonel of the Manchester regiment, stood before the Judge. He had declared at Carlisle to Col. Hamilton "t'would be better to die by the sword than surrender to these damned Hanoverians" - the method of his execution proved the truth of his words.

After Townley, 7 other officers were tried on the following 3 days. The sentence for all "death", but before leaving the Court the ordeal of their end was described to them by the Judge in a cold calculating manner so that they may deliberate their pending execution as they lay huddled in chains in the darkness of their cells.

> "Let the prisoners return to the gaol from whence they came and from thence they must be drawn to the place of execution and when they come there, they must be severally hanged by the neck. But not til they are dead, for they must be cut down alive; then their bowels must be taken out and burned before their faces; then their heads must be severed from their bodies and their bodies severally divided into 4 quarters and these must be at the King's disposal."

There were 46 prisoners brought before the Court and 17 would be executed on Kennington Common. The Manchester officers were the first to be tried; they were also the first to be executed.

On the 30th July there were dragged on wooden sledges onto the field of their pending butchery. The prisoners, bound and pray-

---

* Probably the mass house at Ormskirk. This house became a public house, "The Brewers Arms". A gable end inscription reads 1661 I.E.D. (John Entwistle and wife).

ing, were thrust between the soldiers guarding the wooden structure erected in the centre of the heath. The thousands of spectators hustling and bustling, surging forward yelling to the men, mocking and taunting them in the grotesque carnival atmosphere of the summer's day. The prisoners were bundled up the raised, stage-like platform complete with its scaffold and fiery brazier, the crowd pushing forward, standing on tiptoe for a better view, the newspaper reporters already positioned at the front, quieting the crowd about them fearful that they may miss the last speeches or the gory details of those about to die before them and recording for their appreciative readers the final moments of the dastardly rebels before they were hacked to eternity.

There were similar executions at the cities of York and Carlisle with the same butchery and the same rejoicing. The trials went on throughout that year and into the next. Those who were considered to have led the rebellion were executed. Many of the rank and file were sentenced to transportation. This meant being confined to "hulks". These were old ships which had seen better days, now converted into floating jails, anchored mid-river at the various ports. These vessels would be stocked up with prisoners, sometimes for months, until a transport ship arrived to collect and take them overseas.

There were 936 men, women and children who were pardoned on condition that they went under indentures as bound servants to the plantations of America and the Carribean islands.

However, the Treasury was concerned about the cost of keeping and feeding them prior to organising ships for their departure from Britain.

The English merchants, ever watchful for new markets, quickly spotted the potential of the sale of nearly 1,000 human beings, which incidentally would also enhance their exhibition of patriotism. They were quick to volunteer their services.

By September 1746, 2 merchants had obtained contracts from the government, one a London man Samuel Smith, the other Liverpool Alderman Richard Gildart, whose family were experts at shipping human cargoes across the seas.

The prisoners were bound under indentures to the 2 merchants who then proposed to transfer these indentures at a profit upon reaching the shores of America.

The government would pay the merchants £5 per head for the

transportation cost of each person. Then the merchants would sell the indentures abroad for £7 a head each prisoner consequently worth £12 per individual.

It was not until the spring of 1747 that these prisoners finally arrived in Liverpool. They came from the areas where their trials had taken place, most having already spent over 12 months in various prisons. They were transferred in chains onto the hulk moored in the Mersey. There they remained shackled in pairs in the hold of the ship, awaiting their turn for transportation.

Many were sick and the conditions in the hulk horrendous. It was good fortune, rather than good care, that explained the relatively few deaths, although the seamen of Liverpool were skilful in the art of preserving this kind of cargo.

Mr. Gildart made many complaints and his letters to the authorities expressed concern about the deterioration of his merchandise. On one occasion he suffered a serious loss, a boat containing 8 prisoners being rowed out from the Liverpool quayside to an awaiting vessel struck a rope hawser and capsized. The prisoners, all being shackled together, drowned. Mr. Gildart, of course, wrote to the Treasury requesting his £40 to cover the cost. As his letter explained he had suffered great expense for bedding and provisions and considered that he ought to be compensated for his loss.

The next few weeks saw much to-ing and fro-ing of prisoners, first arriving at the port and then transferring mid-river to the ship that would take them to their final destinations.

One of the last aboard was an Alexander Stewart who had been footman to Prince Charles. He joined 87 other men and women all cramped together in the bowels of the wooden hell ship the "Gildart".

This vessel, owned and operated by the Gildart family, had been joined by the "Johnstown" and other merchant-men all awaiting fair weather, then together they would sail in convoy across the Western Ocean.

In late May 1747, they upped anchor and slipped out of the River Mersey into Liverpool Bay and the Irish Sea, full sail to deliver their human cargoes to a life of bondage in America.

Liverpool's contribution to the conflict probably exceeded that of any other town of comparable size.

When Cumberland and his English forces had been in hot pursuit of the Scots through the North of England, Liverpool had sent

·one of its express riders after them to Carlisle, requesting the needs of the army. The military had asked for biscuit bread and the town of Liverpool responded accordingly, sending a huge supply of 13 wagon loads of biscuit for the troops, Joseph Clegg and William Pole supervising the delivery to the army at Carlisle. The town also sent victuals to the military in Scotland itself.

In the later months of 1745 the Highlands were in the control of the Jacobites and the majority of the forts there held by them, including Fort George at Inverness and Fort August on Loch Ness. Only Fort William on Loch Lunnhe managed to hold out, although by then completely encircled by the rebel forces.

There was no accessible way over the Jacobite controlled mountain roads. The only way to get food supplies through to the besieged garrison forces was by the sea route and through the hazardous narrow straits of the sea loch.

Responding to the desperate situation in the north massive stock piles of supplies of goods for both military and civil aid were deposited at the Port of Liverpool ready to breach the blockade. Liverpool no doubt being selected by the government not only because of its strategic position, but also because of its undisputed loyalty to the Hanoverian cause.

Liverpool ships then ran the gauntlet delivering much needed supplies through the narrows of Carron to the beleaguered forces at Fort William. When the Highlanders withdrew their armies on April 3rd 1746 to converge on Culloden Moor, more ships had arrived to unload the provisions for both troops and civilians for the coming campaign of stabilizing the Highlands.

Liverpool also dispatched cargoes to other ports on the West Coast of Scotland delivering a vast assortment of much needed supplies.

It was these operations that prompted the letters of gratitude to the Corporation from His Majesty the King and His Royal Highness the Duke of Cumberland.

> " .... have on several occasions expressed and testified with Royal gratitude their rememberances of the loyal behaviour of the town of Liverpool ...."

But the town wished for no favours in gratitude for their patriotism and loyalty. But then, they did make one request. Languishing in the Liverpool Tower was a sick rebel prisoner, a Scot by the

2

name of Thomas Lawson*, who had only recently survived an operation for removal of the stone. He had volunteered for Lord Ogilvy's regiment was captured at the fall of Carlisle and tried and condemned to death; then reprieved and sentenced to transportation. Whilst awaiting shipment out to the colonies, he fell ill and underwent an operation. He survived the ordeal but was still not well by January 1749. The Corporation on behalf of the town asked for the release of this man. A reply was received in February and it read:

> Whitehall, 23rd February 1749
> To Joseph Clegg, Mayor of Liverpool

> "The Duke of Bedford hath directed me to acknowledge the receipt of your letter to his Grace of the 14th instant inclosing a petition from Thomas Lawson a rebel prisoner who has been lately cut for the stone at Liverpoole and recommending him to His Grace as a proper object of His Majesty's mercy for a free pardon. I have upon this occassion the satisfaction of informing you that in consideration of your recommendation the King immediately complied with request, making also at the same time the most obliging expressions of his remembering with pleasure the very loyal behaviour of your Corporation during the whole course of the late rebellion. You will be pleased therefore to aquaint the Corporation with this instance of His Majesty's regard forthwith as well as of his goodness and clemensy. And to take the necessary provisions with regard to the poor man until such time as a warrant can be prepared and sent down to Liverpoole to have him discharged in one form."

> Your Most Obedient Servant etc.
> Signed Secretary to the Duke of Bedford

---

* A poor chapman of Alyth, Perth, born at Coupar in Fife

The good news was quickly conveyed to the poor Scot laying in his straw bed at the town jail.

The cell door was flung open and Tom Lawson was assisted to his feet; he stumbled out into the sunlight of Water Street a free man.

• END •

ROYAL WARRANT REGIMENT OF LIVERPOOL BLUES

COLONEL WILLIAM GRAHAM
LT. COLONEL (ALEXANDER) GORDON
MAJOR RICHARD BENDISH

COMPANY	CAPTAIN	LIEUTENANT	ENSIGN
1st	William Tongue	Whittle	Sacheverall
2nd	Laurence Spencer	Walter Shairpe	Halsall
3rd	Peter Mason	Dunbar	Kenyon
4th	Francis Stewart	Matthew Strong	Smith
5th	George Campbell	Wm. Halliday	Wm. Lee
6th	Issac Weakly	John Armitage	Strong
7th	Ben. Heywood	Heyes	Todd
8th	John Colquitt	Joseph Farmer	Dugdale

ADJUTANT - LIEUTENANT DUNBAR
QUARTER MASTER - LIEUTENANT WHITTLE
(ADJUTANT - ENSIGN LEE REPLACED LT. DUNBAR AFTER WIGAN)

Laurence Spencer - Mayor in 1759 - 60)
George Campbell - Mayor in 1763 - 64   )   All were merchants and shipowners
Matthew Strong - Mayor in 1768 - 69   )

Francis Stewart - a tide surveyor   )   Both involved with Customs
Peter Mason - a land waiter   )

John Colquitt - in charge of Customs for the Port (Customs Control Officer)
Ben Heywood (and his brother Ar) - merchants of Hanover Street. In 1774 they received the Royal Assent to become Bankers (Liverpool's First Bank).

114

CHRONOLOGICAL TABLE OF EVENTS

15th August	The Brigantine "Ann" arrives in Liverpool with the news that Prince Charles has landed in Scotland.
16th August	Liverpool express rider sent to London with news of landing.
19th August	Prince Charles raises his standard at Glenfinnan.
4th September	Jacobite army takes Perth.
17th September	Jacobite army takes Edinburgh. Liverpool send loyal address to the King of their support.
21st September	Secretary for War instructs Lords Lieutenants to muster county militias. Jacobites defeat Cope and British forces at Prestonpans. Liverpool requests King's permission to raise own troops.
23rd September	Liverpool receives Royal Sign Manual to raise troops and commission officers.
29th September	"Liverpool Blues" regiment formed. Lord Derby complains about poor state of his county militia and Liverpool's enthusiasm for organising its own troops.
11th October	Completion of commissions now granted to "Liverpool Blues" officers.
28th October	Lord Derby struggling through "red tape" to organise county militia.
10th November	Two of the field officers arrived to take command of the "Liverpool Blues".

14th November	"Liverpool Blues" march out of town to join English forces in the Midlands.
19th November	Advance Jacobite cavalry at Penrith.
23rd November	Lancashire militia march into Liverpool and set up new HQ. Chester Castle and town now fortified. Main body of Jacobite forces at Kendal.
24th November	"Liverpool Blues" receive orders to destroy Warrington Bridge.
25th November	Majority of Jacobite forces at Lancaster.
26th November	"Liverpool Blues" set out to destroy Mersey crossing points.
27th November	Scots army arrive at Preston.
28th November	All bridges over the Mersey destroyed by the "Liverpool Blues"
29th November	Manchester proclaims for Prince Charles and Manchester regiment formed.
1st December	Prince Charles marches out of Manchester. "Blues" ordered to Chester.
4th December	Jacobites at Derby.
6th December	Highland army turns back at Derby.
8th December	Highlanders return to Manchester. Duke of Cumberland and English forces at Litchfield.
10th December	Jacobites at Wigan.
11th December	Cumberland's cavalry at Manchester.
15th December	"Liverpool Blues" arrive at Wigan.

17th December	"Liverpool Blues" at Preston.
18th December	Scirmage at Clifton between Scots Rearguard and English horse soldiers.
19th December	Main body of Jacobites at Carlisle. Cumberland at Penrith.
20th December	Main body of Jacobites cross into Scotland leaving garrison behind at Carlisle.
21st December	Cumberland arrives at Carlisle.
25th December	"Liverpool Blues" take up siege position at Carlisle.
30th December	Carlisle surrenders.
1st January	"Liverpool Blues" return to Liverpool.
14th January	"Liverpool Blues" regiment disbanded.
17th April 1746	Battle of Culloden.

LEADING CHARACTERS
OF THE DAY

HANOVERIANS (OR WHIGS)

BRETHERTON, Thomas
Member of Parliament for Liverpool

BROOMFIELD, James
Mayor of Liverpool - November 1745-1746

BLAND, Major General Humphrey
Commander of troops at Stanwick Bank

CHOLMONDELEY, George Earl of
(Lord Malpas) Lord Lieutenant of Chester and Lord Lieutenant of
North Wales Counties, Governor of Chester Castle

CLEGG, Joseph
Mayor of Liverpool 1748-1749

CUMBERLAND, William Augustus Duke of
2nd son of George II, 1721-1765, Commander of Kings Army

DOUGLAS, Brigadier
On Cholmondeley's Council defending Chester, also "go-between" of
Lord Cholmondeley and the "Blues".

FAWKENER, Everard
Secretary to Duke of Cumberland

HANOVER, George II
King of England from 1727-1760

LIGONIER, Sir John
O. C. of Government forces in South of England

NEWCASTLE, Thomas Pelham-Holles Duke of
First Minister to the King, Secretary of War, Orders from King signed by him

PRITCHARD, Owen
Mayor of Liverpool November 1744 to November 1745

STANLEY, Thomas of Knowsley
Lord Lieut. of Lancashire, C.O. Lancashire Militia

WADE, George Marshall
O.C. of Government forces in North East England (remembered for his military roads in Scotland)

YOUNG, Brigadier Sir William
Acting on behalf of Cholmondeley

STUARTS (OR JACOBITES)

DRUMMOND, Lord John
Brother of Duke of Perth. Landed reinforcements in Scotland from France whilst the Prince was en route through England.

MURRAY, Lord George
Best of all Scottish Field Commanders. Distrusted by Prince because of his independant views.

STUART, Prince Charles Edward
1720-1788. Son of James III and Clemintina Sobieski. "Young Chevalier" to his supporters. "Young Pretender" to Hanoverians.

TOWNLEY, Francis Colonel
5th Son of Charles Townley of Townley in Lancashire. Held a commission in the French Army

PRINCIPAL SOURCES CONSULTED

Account of the Liverpool Blues 1745 by W. Shairpe -
Lv. R. O. (Liverpool Records Office) (Original copy Merseyside Museums)
Collected Papers of the Jacobite Risings Volumes I & II - Rupert
C. Jarvis
Liverpool Town Records - Lv. R. O. (Liverpool Records Office)
Traffords Account Book (Corporation Records) - Lv. R. O.
(Liverpool Records Office)
Derby Letters - Lancashire R. O.
Cholmondeley Letters - Chester R. O.
Occupation of Carlisle - Mounsey

OTHER SOURCES CONSULTED

Battles of the '45 - Tomasson & Buist
Liverpool Privateers and Letters of Marque - Gomer Williams
Memorials of Liverpool - Picton
Liverpool - Professor Muir
Liverpool Shipping - G. Chandler
Liverpools Hidden Story - Stoner
Williamson's Liverpool Memorandum Book
History of Liverpool Volume II - Baines
Culloden - J. Prebble
Transcripts - Dr. Kendrick (28) MS 1008 Warrington
Hale & Orford - Wm Bennett
The Quest Forlorn - C.H. Hartmann
History of Preston - Hardwicke
Compleat History of the Rebellion - James Ray
History of Manchester and Salford - F. A. Bruton
Foundations of Manchester Volume II
History of the Rising - John Home
Old Lancashire - F.O. Blundell
Transcactions of the Lancashire & Cheshire Historial Society
Volumes 5,6,7,17,49,86,91
Lancashire & Cheshire Antiquarians Society Volume LVII
Transactions of the Cumberland & Westmoreland Anti Soc Volume 10
Houghton Papers - Chester R.O.

Public Record Office   State Papers Dom. 69/110
                              State Papers Dom. 75/57
                              State Papers Dom. 75/20 (56)
                              State Papers Dom. 62/63
                              State Papers Dom. 74/61 DRI 37
                              Army Route Books No. 37,
                                        P. 103, 168

Oxfordshire Light Infantry Chronicle for 1801 - C. Denton
George I's Army Volumes I & II - G. Dalton
New Readers Pocket Book 1759
Notes of Wm. Cole 1740
John Brekells Sermons
Ballads & Songs of Lancashire - Harland
Transcripts Relating to Liverpool Volume 2 - A.C. Wardle
Gentleman's Magazine December 1745
Bath Journal December 1745
Chester Courant December 1745
St. Peters (Liverpool) Burial Register
Penrith Burial Register
Aughton Burial Register
Cheadle Burial Register
Churchwardens Accounts for Bickerstaffe
Constables Accounts for Bickerstaffe
Township Accounts for Sefton - T. Williams

List of Illustrations.

BUCKS S.W. PROSPECT OF LIVERPOOL 1728
(From an engraving by Ryland).
Binns Collection.Liverpool R.O

TALBOT HOTEL,WATER ST.LIVERPOOL
Brierley watercolour
Liverpool Record Office

LIVERPOOL TOWER,WATER ST
Binns Collection
Liverpool Record Office

ILLUSTRATION FROM PAGE OF SHAIRPES DIARY
Trustees of the National Museums and Galleries on
Merseyside. Ref. No.DX 594

LETTER FROM SEC OF WAR TO
DEPUTY MAYOR OF LIVERPOOL
Crown Copyright, Control. of HM. Stationery.
Off.PRO

WARRINGTON BRIDGE.
Kendrick illst. Warrington Lib

DEANSGATE,MANCHESTER
Binns Collection
Liverpool Record Office

ST.ANNES SQUARE,MANCHESTER.
(From Casson & Berrys map 1746)
Local Studies Unit. Manchester Central Lib

MR DICKENSONS HOUSE
(From Casson & Berrys map 1746)
Local Studies Unit.Manchester Central Lib

SOUTH PROSPECT,CITY OF CHESTER.1749.
By J.Boydell
Chester Archaeological Soc.& Chester City R.O

CHESTER CASTLE by Moses Griffiths
Grosvenor Museum.Chester

SMITHS MAP OF CARLISLE 1746
Cumbria Record Office (Carlisle)Ref. No.DX334/1

NORTH VIEW OF CARLISLE 1745 By W.H.Nutter
Carlisle Tract
Series.Occupation of Carlisle by G. G. Mounsey

S.W.VIEW OF CARLISLE 1745 By W.H.Nutter
Carlisle Tract

Series.Occupation of Carlisle by G.G.Mounsey

I wish to thank all the above authorities for their assistance and
kind permission in granting the use of the above illustrations.

Author

LIVERPOOL "BLUES" VOLUNTEER 1745 (facing Right) conjectural drawing compiled from Traffords Accounts.Liverpool R.O.&. Shairpes Diary. Liverpool Museums. Front Cover

LIVERPOÒL (BLUES)VOLUNTEER 1745 (facing left) conjectural drawing compiled from Traffords Accounts L.R.O. & Shairpes Diary. Liverpool Musuems.

HIGHLAND SOLDIER conjectural drawing based on contemporary accounts and D.Moriers painting using Scottish prisoners. & Culloden 1746 by A. Heckel

LIVERPOOL BLUES ROUTE MAP